# Lithium Kid

## A Bipolar Adventure From Depression to Mania

**Joshua C. Campo**

# Table of Contents

# Chapter 1:

# Catholic School Shenanigans

Ever since I can remember, I was an antsy, hyperactive, ants-in-your-pants-type of kid. In the early '80s, my family was forced into exile from Managua, Nicaragua to New Orleans, Louisiana. I was only four years old when this happened, so naturally, I didn't have a clue how to speak English.

My family settled in the suburban district of Metairie and enrolled me in a conservative Catholic school called Saint Clement of Rome, which was situated on West Esplanade Avenue. The school was right next to one of the city's smelly drainage canals, which always seemed to flood during storms. The school held mandatory church services for the students once a week. We also had to wear a uniform, which included a little red clip-on tie that we wore only for mass. Though I can't really remember my preschool in Nicaragua, I am certain this school was quite different from what I had just left behind.

Due to my lack of speaking English, my way of communicating was having fun in class with my peers so that I had some connection with them. I still remember the school nuns introducing me to a kid who actually spoke Spanish. That felt like I had just gotten off a spaceship full of Martians and was now back on a common planet, speaking a language I was much more familiar with. In hindsight, that crutch the nuns had given me probably did more harm than good. In the first scenario, with no Spanish-speaking kid around, I bet I would have learned English much faster. After all, I was a hyperactive social butterfly; English was bound to rub off on me.

I guess it didn't though, because at the end of first grade, I went straight to my mother to confess that I had no freaking idea what the hell was going on. This was probably a stupid move because it prompted lots of worry in an already over-stressed mother. Worrying was in her nature; it was like her default setting. If she wasn't worrying, then she was worried that she had nothing to worry about.

My mother was a workaholic, and I've never known why she was that way. My recollection of her was seeing her staying as busy as possible. I bet staying busy was her coping mechanism for something else, which remains a mystery to me. Besides that, her father, who was a dentist-turned-cotton-farmer, was the type to show up to work at 5:30 each morning. For my grandfather, it was a great honor to welcome his workers to the farm at the start of every workday. He spent his entire life working on that farm, up until he passed away at the age of 87. "Retirement" had never been a word he used or mentioned.

One of the ways my mom stayed so busy was by working in real estate, getting involved in the school parenting groups (the PTA), and doing odd things around the house like cleaning closets on Sunday mornings. These were all too commonplace when it came to my mom. There were plenty of closets to clean at my grandmother's big house next to the lake, where we lived with my teenage uncles when we first arrived in the Big Easy.

"For real, Mom," I'd say. "It's 8:00 a.m. and you're in my room, cleaning the closet? Get out of here, you crazy woman." This is something I dealt with until I was old enough to go to college. I still don't understand the urgency of cleaning a closet on a Sunday morning.

So, I graduated from first grade to first grade. It was really rewarding, to say the least. Here I am doing the same grade over again, having to sit in a part of the cafeteria where my friends from the previous year were not sitting. This was damaging for me as a child. I can't explain how it felt, but it planted some inadequacies in me from an early age. In my second go as a first-grader, I was still asking the teacher what the hell was going on. From the cafeteria, I would think, *I'm sitting here but my peeps are sitting over there. Am I being punished for something I didn't do? And, who are these snotty-nosed kids that I'm stuck sitting with now?* I was back on Mars again—twice in one year.

I guess, in the end, it wasn't all that bad to get a whole new batch of kids inside my social circle. Even though I wasn't speaking fluent English yet, I had a knack for making friends. It's always come easy to me, even as an adult, to connect with people. This might be directly related to my various trips to Mars. After all, I got a second chance in first grade to make new friends—not once, but twice. They say you learn 50% of everything you will learn by the age of 6; however, I think I developed a high EQ at a young age out of a sheer need for survival.

I admit, there were very sad moments growing up in my Catholic school. What saddened me the most was that my teachers didn't understand my energy. I was never an ill-intentioned kid or a bully, but I was a Category 5 hurricane most of the time. I was electric, a kid who couldn't sit down. In the adult world, I probably would have been labeled a "crackhead."

Then, there I was, in second grade, with an even better handle on speaking English, but I was still a complete disaster for the teachers. I thought learning should be fun, and when it wasn't, I would just make my own rules. That year, I spent a great amount of time with my face in the corner. That was the punishment for acting out, having fun, and trying to keep my fellow students engaged in what was the most important thing: me. That was one of my coolest years because it was the year I learned I could have a great influence on others.

My father, who was sort of an absent-but-in-the-background kind of guy, took me to the barbershop one day. It was probably a task my domineering, worried mother had assigned him. My father was a smart man; he knew that not following his wife's orders would incur a heavy penalty. He was also a typical Latin American man who had already given up on independence. Fights over what to wear to weddings or other social events like first communions, baptisms—you know, stuff Roman Catholics do—were no longer an issue.

"Set out everything you want me to wear on the bed, honey. I'll start getting ready when you're out of the shower and putting on your makeup," he would tell her. For my dad, getting ready for any important engagement was akin to a genuine work of art. He knew that my mom would take twice as long as he needed, so he had the timing down to a science. And, best of all, he didn't have to think about what tie to wear. *Genius!*

So, anyway, here I am at the barbershop, probably around six years old, and the barber sits me down and bestows great independence on me by asking me—not my father—what kind of haircut I want. "So, what'll it be, son?"

I looked back at my dad, then looked straight into the mirror, and yelled, "Crew cut!"

The barber looked back at my dad with a slight fraction of a laugh and said, "Crew cut? Is that what your son wants?"

I gained a new respect for my dad that day because he didn't do what a lot of parents would have done in that scenario, asking, "You're sure you want a crew cut, son?" That question was never asked. Dad gave me full carte blanche to do as I pleased. With a hint of laughter under his breath, he said, "Crew cut. That's what he said, so that's what he wants." I'm not gonna lie to you: I had no idea what a crew cut was, but it sounded cool, so I went for it.

Some advice on crew cuts, some 40 years later: First and foremost, if you're going to get one, make sure you know what you've got going on underneath your hair. I am one moley dude. I've got moles from my toes to my arms to my chest and back. I even have a bulls-eye mole on my right butt cheek. (This butt mole will come into play later on in this book, so pay attention.)

So, the guy took down my hair in what felt like a matter of seconds. It was soothing and massaging, which is probably not the case for those poor army recruits when they get theirs done without a name and just a seasoned sergeant yelling, "Next!!" That was not my experience. I didn't know what the hell I was getting myself into, but I was sure that I was going to be happy—mostly because I didn't want to look like a wuss in front of my old man. Besides, this was a bonding moment. I never spent time with my dad. (Can you imagine that I never even played catch or went fishing with this guy?) So, the haircut was a big deal—it was a moment of pride, and my father was there to witness it.

It turns out I have moles everywhere, even on my head. I didn't think God made those guys up there. I didn't make anything of it, but it was certainly a curve ball I wasn't expecting. The next day at school was when the fun began. I came into class, guns blazing with my brand-new haircut. I was ready to rock. What I wasn't ready for was what happened next.

I would say most of the class spontaneously burst out laughing, making fun of my haircut. It went in stages: First, people laughed. Then, they wanted to get close to me. And, finally, they all ended up touching my head to get that feeling that only comes from a freshly clipped hairdo. I found the feeling amusing. The only thing that a crew cut was sensitive to was noogies. If a bully got ahold of you, it was going to be rugburn all over your head. Thankfully, the bullies in my class were my allies, so I didn't have to deal with that very much. I don't remember ever feeling embarrassed or regretful of my new hairstyle.

Within two weeks, and after they had all made fun of me and mocked me for my haircut, the entire class of boys had also gotten crew cuts. I felt like a leader, a trendsetter, a pioneer. That is when I realized that people could have great power and influence over others—sometimes, without even trying.

I was sort of ballsy when I was a kid. In New Orleans, I once stuck my foot out so a car could run over it. We were playing in the street at a birthday party for one of our friends, who lived a few blocks over from the townhouse my parents had moved to. Don't ask me what I was thinking; I just wanted to feel what it was like to get your foot run over. I mean, I was crazy and stupid. On that occasion, I broke my toe, but I would still recommend it to anyone who wants to give it a whirl.

The moment the tire went over and off my foot, I felt nothing. I didn't get it. Was I made of steel? Twenty minutes went by and I started crying from the pain. I could feel my heartbeat in my toe. It was totally bizarre! To this day, my family thinks that I accidentally broke my toe, but it was no accident; it was more of an experiment. Remember, I said I had a high EQ, but I never said anything about having a high IQ. That stunt was borderline insane, that's for sure. It was my first taste of insanity and I think I kind of liked it. In the end, I was taken to the emergency room and wound up getting a green fiberglass cast. If anyone has ever had one of those, you'll know that you could go apeshit just from the amount of itching that goes on. My cast reached just shy of my knee, and I had to use a spoon to go deep inside there and scratch away. The thing about scratching an itch is that, sometimes, the more you scratch, the more it itches.

Even though I could speak English by second grade, my energy levels were usually way higher than the other students in my classes. I never considered that what I did was something that stemmed from sin. I was a six-year-old boy, how bad could I be? I don't even remember why I was sent to the corner half the time, but I can tell you that I spent a lot of time there.

My mother, who was very involved in the school since both my older brother, William and I went there, would visit often. She would come into my class and ask the teacher, "Where is my little boy?" I, of course, was in the same corner, which was pretty much my new home at this point. This was a standing deal, meaning there was no sitting allowed when you were sent to the corner, so it sucked. But, I didn't know any better and that was the best way for the teacher to handle my unruly disposition.

My mom recalls one day when she was at the school because they were planning the annual school fair. This was a big event, one that the school prided itself on. The kids loved it because it involved a tradition where you would buy confetti-filled eggshells and sneak up on your friends to greet them with a not-so-polite confetti egg to the noggin. My mom was in a room, sorting out details, when a mother came in and said, "Oh my God! There is this boy, he's such a troublemaker. He's a nightmare."

My mom, who was sitting with the group of room mothers, grew curious. "What is this boy's name?"

"Joshua," said the lady.

My mom's shoulders dropped as she confessed, "That's my little boy."

During that year, I had a nun who fell in love with me. She saw that I was a good-natured child, the love that I had to give, and how misunderstood I was. Sister Claire was very special to me. Her affection kept my self-esteem in check. After all, if a nun could see the good in me, then I wasn't half as bad as the teachers were making me out to be.

Beyond the time-outs at the corner, I would also regularly receive notes written by my teacher, which she so nicely stapled to my shirt. I never read them, but I assume they were a play-by-play of what I had conjured up as the offense of the day. At the end of the day, Sister Claire would come up to me with her loving arms and gently take the paper from my shirt. "Joooshieee," she would say in her dry Gaelic gait, "Tomorrow, you are going to be good, right?"

Of course, my answer was, "Yes, Sister Claire, I promise."

I don't recall things ever getting better for me. I was a hyper kid. I probably needed a double dose of PE; maybe then I could find some sense of calm. I bet in today's world I would have been diagnosed with ADHD and put on a daily regimen of some type of mind-numbing drug. Knowing that this is so mainstream today makes me sad. I mean, sure, some kids need it, but it also seems like it's completely overprescribed—almost as if it's a quick fix. Who knows what I would have been prescribed at the time.

At the end of second grade, my parents had important news for us: We were moving from New Orleans to Miami. *What the hell?* Another loss of friends after all that I'd done to make some? I had already acquired an army of bald cadets who were loyal to their leader. Obviously, I didn't see it that way, but come on! I had to go through this again? For real? New place, new school, *and* new friends?

I don't know—I mean, I really didn't know how this was going to turn out. I wasn't scared, but I wasn't excited either.

Chapter 2:

# Nicaragua and Moving to the US

My parents are Nicaraguan. They loved their home country, but things had gotten too difficult for them to live there. Nicaragua was used to being ruled by dictators or even dynasties, where fathers in power would pass that power down to their sons. This reached a boiling point when Anastasio Somoza, the leader of the dynastic family at the time (late 1970s), decided to pilfer most of the aid that was received to help the country surmount the death and destruction caused by a terrible earthquake in 1972.

The natural disaster virtually leveled the capital city of Managua, killing around 10,000 people and leaving more than 300,000 homeless. Guerrilla movements and clandestine organizations that were planning to overthrow Somoza were already active, but this didn't reach a critical mass until the assassination of Pedro Joaquin Chamorro in 1978. Pedro Joaquin was important because he was a prominent opposition journalist from a well-known Nicaraguan family, who also owned the nation's largest newspaper, *La Prensa.*

No one really knows who was behind the gruesome murder, as Pedro was behind the wheel of his car when he was gunned down by several assailants with the use of multiple shotgun rounds. Some even claim that the opposition did it to spark discontent with Somoza. From what I know, the truth was never revealed to the public, but most fingers pointed at Somoza.

I was born in 1978, the same year the revolution exploded in Nicaragua. Gunfights on street corners, whole cities being taken over, aerial bombing assaults from Somoza's air force, kidnappings, point-blank executions from both sides—all of this was commonplace. It was a difficult time for Nicaraguans, a dangerous time. However, Somoza was finally overthrown and the promise of democracy was at hand.

The exact date the revolution successfully overthrew the Somoza dynasty was July 19, 1979. This date is extremely important for those who opposed Somoza as well as Nicaraguans living in exile at that time. There is a long explanation about what transpired, but I don't want to get into that here. It will turn this book into a political piece with a slant that will either go left or right, so for now, let's just keep it in the middle. The most important thing to understand is that with the revolution came sweeping changes to the business and social fabric of the whole country. Some reforms were celebrated worldwide, as they were changes designed to help Nicaragua's humble and needy population, which made up the vast majority of its citizens. An example of positive change was a national campaign that was put in place to eradicate illiteracy on a national level.

Granted, I was a baby in the 1980s, so I will plead the fifth as to whether things that happened during this time were good or bad for Nicaragua. What I can say is that, by 1982, my parents had grown disillusioned with the situation and made the decision to leave the country. I know that this was something they did with a heavy heart. Nicaragua was their home, a country that has been a part of my family tree, spanning back generations.

There, my parents were well-known. Nicaragua, after all, is a small country, with it being about the size of the U.S. state of Georgia and its population of what must have been around 3 million souls back then. Last names, both the father's and mother's, still carry a lot of weight in this society. In the US, however, we were "nobodies," just a social security number. My father still looks back today and feels like the revolution robbed him of his most productive years. It has always been a sore spot in his memory.

So, sometime around 1986, we moved from New Orleans to Miami. My parents were very much a middle-class family, trying to make ends meet. We no longer went to a private or Catholic school. My first academic experience in Miami was at a public elementary school called Calusa. Named after the Calusa tribes that once inhabited that part of Florida, our neighborhood was set against a lush golf course, surrounded by beautiful, immaculately landscaped mansions.

We lived within walking distance of my new school, in a small townhouse community called Calusa Point. I have only fond memories of those years at Calusa. The elementary school had a special aura I can't put into words. It was a place of happiness and positive role models. I don't remember the names of any of my teachers, but I do remember some of the girls that I "dated" while I was there.

Even though I was only, maybe, seven years old, I had girlfriends. I remember on several occasions, having one particular girlfriend, who was in another class, come to the bathroom, which was shared between the two classrooms. There was a girls' bathroom and a boys' bathroom, and I would pass by her class and signal a kiss by touching my two fingers to my lips so she knew to ask her teacher for a bathroom pass. We never French kissed—I was way too young to even know what that was—but it was still exhilarating, a rush of blood transported to my lips as they touched hers.

During those years, I wound up dating two beautiful twin girls from Venezuela, Marianela and Andreina. I dated the first one, got bored, and started dating the other. That was pretty crazy at the time. While all the boys in my grade were busy beating up the girls they liked, I was busy kissing them.

I don't know why I was somehow different, but I was. Calusa was a very friendly environment, where meeting new people was easy. By the time I got to this school, my hyperactivity had toned down a bit. I mean, it was always there, but I guess the girls and all that kissing helped me keep it in check.

Calusa Point was also good for my hyper disposition because my parents felt like the neighborhood was safe. I could ride my bike around, go almost anywhere, and encounter hardly any cars. It also had things we considered "luxuries" at the time, such as tennis courts and a pool house. It was a wonderful bubble, but I suspect my father was not any happier. He truly missed Nicaragua; it was a country he held close to his heart.

# Chapter 3:

# Small-Time Crook and a New Address

One time, I spent the entire day on my bike. It must have been on a weekend. That day, I was rolling with my regular posse, but we ended up meeting some new kids who didn't go to Calusa. I guess they were a bad influence on us because that was the day I became a small-time criminal.

We went around my neighborhood and beyond, looking for luxury cars, which aren't difficult to find in Miami, as many people own extremely expensive cars. With the cars I went for, I didn't even think what I was doing was stealing at all. I somehow convinced myself that swiping metal tire gauges—you know, those little twisty things that come on each tire and are usually made of plastic—off cars like Porsches or BMWs was okay.

Unfortunately, the act of stealing from one car only ignited my desire to steal more. The more I stole, the more I wanted to steal. It got to the point where we had probably hit up to 10 or more cars. My friends, old and new, were jubilant as we increased our stash. I think what made it fun was that we all knew, deep down, that what we were doing was wrong.

After a day of stealing metal tire gauges, we were tired. One of the guys told us that we should come over to his house and eat. So, the crew showed up to his house, probably 40 metal gauges deep. We had them in cloth bags, and the gauges were distributed into four bags so that each kid could have his own bag. Upon getting to my friend's house, we got busted big time.

My friend's mother was aware of what we had done. She accused us and treated us like criminals. She said she would call the cops on us. *Damn*, I thought. *I didn't know that I could go to jail for this.* The floor beneath me collapsed as I was shaken by this new turn of events. The mom was bluffing but wanted to teach all of us an important lesson in respecting other people's possessions. To be completely honest, I never stole another thing in my life again, so, perhaps, it was a good lesson to learn.

After living in Calusa Point for a couple of years, my parents must have saved some money because they purchased a rundown home in a nice neighborhood in Miami, just east of US-1. My mom could see what was more difficult for my father to see. She had been a real estate agent all her life—she even worked as a realtor when we lived in Nicaragua. She had a vision for the house and how it would be transformed. I guess her passion was so strong that she was able to convince my father that this was a house that we could live in for the rest of our lives.

The house seemed very dark when I first went to see it. This avocado-green carpet with circular shapes in gold-covered floors was straight out of the '60s. Not only was the carpet hideous but it had also accumulated years and years of dust. The darkness was not a permanent situation; there were two huge plastic curtains that were probably put there so no one could peer into the house. Once you drew the curtains, light would flood the place.

The house had both a huge front yard and backyard, which is what Mom was paying attention to. It sat right smack in the middle of what seemed to be an acre of land. I don't know if it was an acre or a half-acre. When you're just a kid, everything looks like an acre. There were two enormous pine trees in the front, as well as a big flowering tree in the back that would shed leaves and flowers 24/7. That tree became the bane of my brother's existence, as his chore list included raking up the discarded leaves and petals in order to receive his allowance. That tree was also transformed into a treehouse that my father lovingly crafted for my little sister, Catalina.

A new house meant a new public school because we were now in a different district. This time around, I didn't even flinch. My attitude was that I could make friends wherever I went. I wasn't worried. Besides, it was going to be fun: new school, new friends, *and* new girls.

It's funny that I even bring up the subject of Nicaragua. In all honesty, I didn't even realize I was Nicaraguan until my family made a visit there in the summer of 1991, which was a time of change in the national politics of the country. My father, who never felt he fit in in the US, was anxious to return to his country. As for my mother, that was a different story.

My mother was happy with our life in Miami. We owned a nice home, her children went to great public schools, and our life was good. We had stability and things—well, things weren't broken. And, if it ain't broke, don't fix it. (This is one of my favorite American sayings—I would say it's as American as sliced bread and apple pie, hahaha.)

So, needless to say, there was a bit of friction on pushing this decision to leave Miami after having made a life there for more than half a decade. Packing up and moving back to the country we both loved and hated was bittersweet. I can safely say that when it came to day-to-day activities, I come from a matriarchy; but, when it came to the big decisions, my father was in charge. I think, in his mind, my father was already dead set on going back to his homeland. However, I bet, knowing my mother, that they had agreed to spend a summer there before making the final decision.

That was the summer of 1991, when it finally dawned on me that I was Nicaraguan. I mean, I knew where it was on a map, I could speak Spanish, I knew we had some traditional cuisine, and I also knew what the flag looked like; but beyond that, I didn't know much. That summer, I was somehow under the impression that we were moving there. I even broke up with my girlfriend at the time and told her I was moving away. That's what my parents were telling me, but I guess I misunderstood what was going on because we went down there for the summer and came back for one more year of school in Miami.

During the four years living at our new address in Miami, I went to three different schools. The first one was an elementary school called Howard Drive, where I attended fourth and fifth grades. I believe that it was at this time that I was introduced to the saxophone. My parents, who both played music, actively encouraged all their children to take up an instrument. My oldest brother, William, played the French horn. He had started on the trumpet back in the New Orleans days and switched instruments at some point along the way. He took it very seriously and even went on to study music at the university level. My other older brother, Francisco, took up the alto clarinet. This was a very strange instrument because it looked more like a sax and was rare to see in classical or contemporary music. I chose the alto saxophone—something about its curves and sound literally hit a chord.

At that time, I became a news anchor for the morning minutes at school. Every classroom at Howard Drive had a television, and every morning, we would read the morning announcements. My co-anchor's name was Ronnica. She was a sweet and spunky girl who enjoyed reading the news as much as I did.

There was an incident that I will never forget that happened to Ronnica and me. We were reading the lunch menu of the day. It's important to note here that we were used to saying things like "macaroni and cheese," "pizza boats," and "lasagna"—things you normally encounter at a public school cafeteria. Well, one time, the menu said something like "potatoes au gratin." When we read the day's menu, both Ronnica and I started to crack up with laughter. We couldn't stop ourselves. Here, we were on live TV, and I was peeing in my pants having a laughter attack at "potatoes au gratin." It was hilarious mostly because it was both of us laughing our asses off, and we knew that we weren't supposed to, which made it even more difficult to stop.

The second school I went to is what I believe to have been some sort of social experiment. The issue was that my elementary school and others like it only offered grades 1 through 5. Middle school came after elementary school, and it covered grades 7 to 9. So, basically, they took us to a school in an area of Miami called Richmond Heights, which was a predominantly black neighborhood, and bussed in several elementary schools, with all the students representing sixth grade. I thought it was the coolest experiment because I became friends with new people. Just imagine a school with close to 300 sixth graders. That was a freaking awesome experience! The school was called FC Martin and, like I said before, it was a large school that received students from all over the city.

The FC Martin days were bittersweet. I had a huge crush on a girl who I would only see pass by or from afar. In other circumstances, I would have been in a class with her, but that was not the case here. There were so many students of the same age and grade that it would have been impossible for all of them to meet one another. What was also kind of weird about this school was that the students they put you with weren't even necessarily from your elementary school or geographical area. So, you made friends, but then by the end of the academic year, it was time to say goodbye for good.

I don't really understand why elementary school didn't just go through sixth grade. The whole experience was bizarre, but I wouldn't change a thing about it. This school made me even more adaptable. I learned to make friends so easily that I didn't even worry about the next school or the next challenge.

PMS—that was the name of my new school: Palmetto Middle School. I don't remember ever riding my bike to school, as I had done when I attended both Calusa and Howard Drive. I know I didn't ride to school in sixth grade because the school was too far away from where I lived. I think that, in the case of Palmetto, we were just dropped off each morning. Getting a ride home was pretty annoying, though.

My mom was a real estate agent. As an adult now, I understand what that means because I, too, have worked in real estate. What's important to note about people who work in this industry is that you are not in complete control of your time. You often find yourself taking longer than what you had planned, especially if you're about to close on a sale. Having said that, my mother was late to pick us up *a lot.*

In the beginning, I would get kind of annoyed, but I was never a diva about it. She was doing an honest job, and that is something I always admired about her. So, I guess you can say hanging out those extra hours after school wasn't so bad.

Chapter 4:

# Sax and Sweetheart of the Year

At some point, under the influence of my oldest brother, William, I started to take saxophone lessons after school with his marching band and jazz band teacher, Mr. Walker. This took place at Palmetto High School, aka PHS. I still remember those long walks, carrying my sax from PMS to PHS.

Mr. Walker was a black man with magnetic charisma. I was very fond of him. He was the real deal: an excellent saxophone player and a really cool and easy-going guy. I probably took lessons with Mr. Walker for at least 6 months. Later on, I found out that Mr. Walker had been incarcerated after having been accused and found guilty of statutory rape. Apparently, he was having sex with female students from the school. But, beside the fact that Mr. Walker got sent to prison, I still hold great memories of him as a person and mentor.

I was in seventh grade that year. My younger sister, Catalina, always joked and said that that was the apex of my life. The highest point: I was popular, I did well in school, I was a badass on the sax, and I was getting really good at tennis. Somewhere in the thick of seventh grade, I had accumulated an army of friends. My average morning consisted of me giving out 15 hugs to all my friends before getting to class. I also had a ton of girlfriends to choose from—or, at least, it felt that way.

That year, which was 1992, I was crowned "Sweetheart" of my grade, a prize that was pretty much given to the most popular person. Seventh, eighth, and ninth grades each had their prince and princess, which was awarded on Valentine's Day. My princess was Amber Goldberg, a gorgeous, sweet Jewish girl from my grade.

All of the Sweethearts had to report to center stage for a ceremonial dance. Amber was one of the biggest crushes I ever had, and I had the biggest hard-on during that whole dance. It was so big that I couldn't comfortably dance with her. I had been crushing on this girl since the beginning of middle school, and now I had her in front of me. All I know is that I couldn't take the pressure, so I couldn't seal the deal. I was totally intimidated. I wanted her so bad that I felt like I had pocket aces in a game of Texas Hold'em. Although, looking back, I know I totally played my cards all wrong.

Believe it or not, I think I would have had much better chances if we had not won Sweetheart of the Year. It was too much pressure. I wanted to kiss her, but the whole school was watching. It's kind of like when you're at a wedding and an old aunt tells you to go ask Cousin Steph to dance. When that happens, the opposite effect occurs—your desire to dance was just heisted by an aunt who wouldn't mind her own freaking business. It got even worse when my father started introducing me to the hottest single girl at a wedding, for example, by telling her I'm single—which is basically code for your dad calling you a loser without him even knowing it. Parents like my dad are the kings of messing things up for me socially. The worst part is that, in their heads, they're being social philanthropists, cupids, and matchmakers while they are actually setting fire to the Hindenburg.

Something I've learned about women over my years of practice in trying to get a girl's interest is that, as you try courting them, there's usually only a small window of opportunity when they look at you and you have a chance to go up to bat. That narrow moment of time is so delicate that you have to pick your words and actions carefully. When a woman gives you a chance, you have a very small amount of time. If you try to get physical too early on, or if you say or do something that might be construed as offensive to them, then that window closes and your chances to re-engage vanish almost completely.

When it comes to meeting new people, I've always noticed that it's better to meet and try to get together with a new girl, someone you don't know at all, than trying to get something going with a girl you already know. Sometimes, getting out of the friend zone is more difficult than escaping Alcatraz. I also follow a general rule about meeting new people, whether they're a guy or a girl.

The way I look at it, everybody you encounter in life is either a tunnel, a bridge, or a road. Allow me to explain: A tunnel is someone you meet who may end up being toxic for you. It's a tunnel because you get in and out very fast. This includes one-night stands that don't turn into friendships and, instead, become people you'd rather avoid. Tunnels can be friends who are alcoholics or drug addicts who don't really add much to your life, for example.

A bridge is someone you meet in your life whom you sustain a positive relationship with and likely introduces you to new people. Bridges are probably the most important of the three infrastructures I mentioned. After all, a bridge can introduce you to another bridge, and that bridge might introduce you to another bridge, and so on. Bridges are not exempt from introducing you to tunnels or roads. Roads are the most valuable of the three, however, because they are the hardest to find. Roads are people who will be your friends for the rest of your life. These are the friends you can consider your chosen family. You stay in touch with some on a regular basis; others you don't speak with for years, but when you see each other again, it's like no time has passed at all.

I've learned to live by these rules because I truly believe that everyone you run into in life has a purpose for existing. And, yes, you will run into narcissistic egomaniacs who believe that they are the sun and that all the planets revolve around them. Then, there are gossip queens or kings who have nothing better to do than to talk about other people's lives.

I love people, both new and old, because most of them add positive energy to my life. I've tried to surround myself with these kinds of people, but it can be tricky. I've learned to create a shield against toxic people and see it as an opportunity to build tolerance. It's a fine art to tolerate things that really get under your skin and, unfortunately, life is not all sunflowers and rainbows. Sometimes, you have to learn to put on some sunscreen and protect yourself.

Chapter 5:

# Moving Back to Nicaragua

Seventh grade was my last year at PMS. That summer was the second summer we went to Nicaragua, only, this time, we were buying one-way tickets. The summer before was way different than the next. Last time around, we were kind of just horsing around, going to the beach, and taking in the scenery, some of which was really difficult to take in. The only guidebook that covered Nicaragua at the time described the capital as "uglier than ugly and hotter than hell." *Yikes!* That's a little rough, but not too far off the mark.

Every traffic light was crawling with beggars, window cleaners, or mothers begging while they held their babies in the sweltering Managua heat. That experience, seeing all that as a child, changes a person. You no longer take your privileged life for granted. These people at the traffic lights were just the surface. If you really wanted to find out what was going on, you had to go into the slums—something I've never done out of fear.

That summer, which was when we decided to move back to Nicaragua for good, I discovered some really cool things about the place. First off, being 13 essentially made you an adult. My friends and I could readily purchase and drink alcohol and buy smokes if we wanted. This started happening when we were in our second semester of eighth grade. Who could blame us? There were, after all, no other forms of entertainment—no malls, no cinema, not even a McDonald's. The country was a complete wreck trying to recover from a decade of revolution, followed by a civil war and hyperinflation.

At first, we all held the dubious distinction of just about everyone being millionaires in local currency. You would ask the seller how much, and they would just answer "five," to which you'd have to reply, "Five-hundred thousand, fifty thousand, or five million?"

One of the first things that affected me every morning when we got to Managua was taking cold-ass showers. The water would come from on high and was fed to us basically by gravity from the house's individual storage tank, which was perched above the roof. It was *so* cold, in fact, that you'd know whenever someone was taking a shower by the inevitable scream you'd hear as they braved that Antarctic chill for the first time every morning.

I didn't realize how coddled I was when we lived in Miami. We had central air conditioning and hot water, but in Nicaragua, we had neither of those things. Believe me, this was hard on me as a kid. But, in hindsight, it taught me a valuable lesson: "Suck it up, kid. Stop being a drama queen." Now, my little sister was only six years younger than me and was always my sidekick. She was seven when we moved and the water situation was too much for her, so they would heat water for her and mix it in a barrel so she didn't have to visit Siberia every morning. In Latin America, being the only girl means having some privileges that the boys didn't get.

On a side note, I had never seen such amazing natural beauty than what I would encounter during my time there. Nicaragua is a tropical paradise. Just from Managua, you could witness spectacular views. One that I'm particularly fond of is a huge volcano called Momotombo that towers above a smaller one called Momotombito. Both volcanoes are near-perfect cones, and both are on or next to Lake Managua (on, in Momotombito's case, as it is actually an island inside the lake).

The view coming into the city from the main highway featured these volcanoes and the lake. It was simply breathtaking. You see a beautiful lake in the foreground, and both volcanoes behind it in perfect unison, with the small volcano directly in front of the big one, plus an aquamarine lagoon in between called Laguna de Xiloá. For those who don't know, a lagoon is essentially an old volcano whose crater has filled with water over thousands of years. It turns out that lagoons are more likely to be formed in more ancient volcanic areas. Hawaii, for example, is considered a new volcanic area while Central America is considered older, geologically speaking.

Managua, the capital, suffers immensely from urban sprawl due to two events that happened in the city's past. First, there was the earthquake of 1972, which decimated most of the city. The old capital was built in colonial style, which made it not only a lot denser but also more appealing. Like most old cities in Latin America, Managua was designed to have pedestrians and transit merging together in perfect harmony. I assume that old Managua was probably something like Havana, Cuba.

The new city spread out away from the fault lines that riddled the ruins of the former center. Poor construction methods and a lingering fear of earthquakes compounded by the economic effects of civil unrest meant practically no vertical housing. The resulting low-rise suburban sprawl of modest tin-roofed homes immersed in greenery gives the current city a farm-with-an-airport feel.

The city's creation is an interesting case of coming to a national compromise. Much of Nicaragua's history is riddled with internecine warfare between its formerly largest, oldest, and most important cities: Leon and Granada. These two cities duked it out constantly to settle which one would be Nicaragua's coveted capital. After countless wars, spanning more than a century, it was decided that Managua—which was situated nearly halfway between Leon and Granada—would be the permanent compromise spot for the capital city.

All the cities at that time were next to a body of water—Granada had Lake Nicaragua and both Leon and Managua were on the shores of Lake Managua. The exact location of Leon would change after a volcanic eruption and earthquakes destroyed the city. Today, Leon is about a 75-minute drive from the capital, while it takes around 45 minutes to reach Granada from Managua. An interesting side note is that Granada is one of the oldest, if not *the* oldest, colonial cities on the American mainland (founded in 1524). This does not include colonial settlements on Caribbean islands. There are several in that region that are a bit older.

Chapter 6:

# A Special Beach Called Poneloya

My first love when I moved to Nicaragua was the beach. I had come from Miami, where we would spend most of our beach trips in either Fort Lauderdale or Fort Myers. Fort Lauderdale was on the east side of Florida and was a relatively close driving distance for us from Miami. It was a place where we would coordinate with other Nicaraguans who were close friends of my parents and do day trips.

The idea was to get to Fort Lauderdale early enough to claim a shady picnic table. From there, the table became our beachhead. There was always some adult from the group either sitting there or hanging close by to protect our stuff. And, there were always these small annoying pinecones about the size of a marble that would wreak havoc on your feet if you weren't wearing flip-flops on the jaunt down to the water. The end of the beach fringed the Port Everglades shipping channel, meaning, every once in a while, we would catch a glance of a massive cruise ship or a scary submarine passing very close by on their way out to sea.

Fort Myers was a whole other story. We would only go there when we took long vacations and had time to stay over for three or four nights. This beach was situated on the opposite side of the peninsula from Fort Lauderdale, on the Gulf of Mexico, on the west coast of Florida. Getting there probably took around four or five hours.

Our living quarters were unpretentious but spectacular. We would rent an old wooden house right on the sand. It was built on low stilts, giving us a sandy playpen underneath where we would make sandcastles in the shade and sometimes even prop up tents and camp out overnight. Days were spent on the beach right in front of the house, and we spent most of our time swimming, collecting starfish, and taking the odd trip over to the pier to do some people-watching or reading funny keychains in the souvenir shops.

The beaches in Nicaragua, however, were simply stunning. First and foremost, we were now on the Pacific Ocean. Now, the waves were much bigger on average than what we were used to seeing in Florida. As a teenager, I was inspired by these waves. In the first half of the '90s, we stayed at my mother's brother's home. The house was left behind in the wake of an airplane accident that killed my uncle when he was only 33 years old. His name was Ofilio, like my grandfather. My mother said her brother was extremely bright and even thought of him as almost supernatural in some ways.

Uncle Ofilio was that guy who lived too fast and was always on the edge. He had actually gotten into an automobile accident as a teenager while he was drinking and driving, resulting in one of his passengers, a girl, ending up dead. My grandfather came from a family where there was no such thing as a free lunch. Uncle Ofilio was told by his father, my grandfather, that he was not welcome in his home. My grandfather continued by saying, "You are guilty of killing a person. You need to go to prison and pay off your debt to society for doing this."

My mom recalls this as one of the most difficult times for the family. In the end, it all paled in comparison to Ofilio's death in a solo plane crash. It turns out that many instruments that are commonplace in a two-seater Cessna were out of commission or not calibrated correctly. The farm was large enough that it had its own landing strip. Who knows what kind of maintenance regiment they were putting the crop-dusters through; but if it was anything like typical Nicaraguan style, it was surely on the more relaxed end of the spectrum. Uncle Ofilio had gone up in the plane because there were some bandits stealing cotton, the main crop that our family grew during those times. He circled above the white-speckled fields and, apparently, got too close to the ground. As a result, the plane ran out of air, stalled, and then crashed. He died immediately on impact.

The impact of Ofilio's death on my mother was so strong that she was too shocked to even cry. She would always say that she cries at movies but that it's all different in real life. It's interesting because my mother says she doesn't go to cemeteries; she believes there's no point in living in the past.

After Uncle Ofilio's death, his widow, Aunt Sandra, moved back to El Salvador, where her family had settled years earlier. My grandfather decided to help her by taking over the maintenance and everything else related to the beach house. It was understood to be Sandra's house, but the ones who would enjoy it for the next decade or so would be my grandparents and my mother's siblings, her kids, and their kids (our first cousins).

The house was a modern green-and-white one-story concrete core with bedroom suites, surrounded by open living space on three sides. The exterior walls consisted of pillars connected by horizontal slats of wood to give minimal privacy while allowing the ocean breezes to circulate. It was right on the sand. When we moved back to Nicaragua, there were a couple of years when we actually spent the entire summer on the beach in Poneloya. I have such fond memories of that little town. I learned how to live a full beach life, needing nothing more or less. It was also here that I almost lost my life to the sea. Poneloya has a reputation for having the country's most treacherous surf.

The day I almost died in the ocean is one that I'll never forget. I had decided to dip my toes in for a bit to see if the waves were working well for boogie-boarding. The ideal wave for both a surfer and boogie-boarder is the same: You want a clean wave that breaks from one side to the other. The opposite is a big wave, where the whole line of water just falls at the same time. A wave that breaks from one side to another allows for horizontal movement on the water's surface. Because Nicaragua has a huge lake, Lake Nicaragua, measuring 8,264 km$^2$ (just a bit smaller than Puerto Rico, at 9,104 km$^2$), the wind tends to travel from lake to the ocean, creating very clean waves with offshore winds almost 300 days a year.

So, I was swimming to scan the waves while facing in the direction of the ocean. I could swear that not even 10 minutes had passed when I turned around and realized that I was very far from shore. The houses looked like a surreal painting of tiny huts on the horizon. At this point, I was frightened. It's crazy how the mind works because I wasn't worried about drowning so much as I was about the idea that a shark would end up having me for lunch. In that moment, I panicked.

Panicking is the fastest way to lose energy quickly. I couldn't scream—the surf was too loud for anyone to hear it anyway. All I could do was wave my arms. I think, by that point, I had already swallowed some saltwater and was becoming weaker. An uncle of mine, who also loved boogie-boarding, spotted me from shore in the distance. The next thing I remember was him crunching his body to mine and the board.

I was spent. I couldn't even move to help us along. From there, I blacked out. I can't remember getting back to the coast. My uncle was a hero. Even to this day, I always make sure to give him a big hug when I see him.

Poneloya was the beach that my mother's side of the family had frequented their whole lives. That made perfect sense, considering that the city they were from, Leon, is just a 15-minute drive away. Everyone in my family knew the rules when it came to this beach. At high tide, the undertow going down is quite serious, partly because the ocean is infused with an uneven floor, and, between the coast and the beach, there is a pretty vicious diagonal drop. This is what I believe causes the undertow.

The rules were pretty simple: No one is allowed in the water by themselves. The idea was that if someone got caught in the undertow, the other person would signal for help. There were small fishing boats in the shallow harbor at the end of the beach that you could easily get to and save the drowning person. I've learned over time that it's better to go in when it's low tide going up rather than high tide coming down. There's far more undertow in the latter than the former.

Having said that, I never once saw someone flagging for help or a boat going out for a rescue; however, I have heard stories about people drowning in Poneloya. This was especially true during peak holidays between Christmas, New Year's, and during Holy Week, which is the week leading up to Easter Sunday. On these dates, crowds of people from all over the country would pack the beach and get absolutely smashed drunk. Some would give in to temptation and decide to cool off with a dip in the water. Being inebriated and navigating Poneloya's treacherous surf do not go well together, especially if you haven't the slightest clue how to swim in the first place. As a result, there were always reports of people drowning during these holidays.

There was one story I'll never forget that had to do with a principal at the American Nicaraguan School. This was the elite school of Nicaragua at the time. It was kind of a prep school where most of the wealthiest families enrolled their kids. The school principal had gone to Poneloya on a random weekend with a canine company in tow. It turns out the dog went for a swim and got caught in a current that pulled him out to the open sea. The principal, whose name I don't recall, raced in to save his companion, but both were lost to the ocean. It was a tragic story and one that I will never forget when braving Poneloya's unpredictable surf.

Chapter 7:

# High School Years at ANS

Part of the reason I knew about the story of the ill-fated principal and his dog was because I also went to school at ANS (American Nicaraguan School). School there was very different from the public schools in Miami. The first thing to note, which I haven't yet mentioned, is that, in Nicaragua, I was related to half the people I knew—no joke. A significant number of people were distant cousins or aunts and uncles.

My first year there was, when I was in eighth grade, it was essentially a school for the richest kids in Nicaraguan society. I knew that I, somehow, belonged to this socially constructed "upper class," but I also knew that my parents didn't have the type of money that most of my classmates did. "If you can't make it, fake it" was the motto of the moment.

My first year at ANS was rough. I found that some people were distant and kind of snooty. Despite my charisma, making friends became much more difficult than before. I do have to recognize, in hindsight, that we were at the age when we were all going through puberty, so everyone was just a little funky. During my first year, it was challenging to make a lot of friends. Some of my classmates came from millionaire families, which I think affected their egos and made it more difficult to connect. I honestly never knew much about my parents' finances, but if we were rich, they sure made it seem like we weren't.

ANS was a strange school because its high-school classrooms, which ranged from grades 8 to 12, had walls and ceilings that were made of these improvised corrugated metal plates. It turns out that these buildings weren't so much classrooms as they were reminiscent of torture chambers. It got so hot in there some days that it would be well above 100°F. The classrooms were meant to be provisional and were built after the earthquake of '72, which had destroyed the original school. Who knows where the funds to build real classrooms had gone, because it was 1992, 20 years later, and we were still roasting in these provisional ovens where we were expected to learn.

The worst of the day was going to PE and having to change in a hurry to get back to class. Periods were only 45 minutes long, which made it an enormous pain in the ass to play soccer or any other sport. This meant changing, playing, and changing back all within that short timeframe. On top of that, the school made us wear uniforms. They were generally okay because they were kind of casual. We were allowed the uniform shirt, blue jeans, and pretty much any shoe we wanted, which were usually tennis shoes because it made no sense to be lugging around dress shoes when you had PE every day. What I couldn't stand were the teachers who made you tuck in your shirt. Believe me, there's a temperature difference when you're coming back from exercising and drenched in sweat. Leaving the shirt untucked allowed us to breathe some of the heat out, whereas tucking it in would seal the heat to our bodies. A couple of times, after taking a test in PE, I literally turned in a wet piece of paper. I mean, what we all went through was inhumane.

Ninth and tenth grades whizzed by. I didn't have a ton of friends, but by this time I had reconciled with the fact that friends were about quality, not quantity. I was happy with the people who had become my friends. I don't know if I was one of the cool kids, but by this time my mind was on sports, grades, and girls, and I was doing okay in all three departments.

In sports, the United States hosted the 1994 World Cup. Watching the games inspired me to join the soccer team. During those times, I would play soccer during PE and then stay on after school for team practice. Watching the World Cup made me believe that I, too, could be a great soccer player. I wasn't. All I could offer my team was speed and endurance. I couldn't dribble a ball to save my life. Naturally, I was put on defense, though, of course, I wanted what every kid wanted: to be a forward or even a midfielder, score some goals, and become a hero.

Where grades were concerned, I was always a solid B+/A- student. Not the top of my class, which was approximately 100 of us, but maybe around the top 20%—which was okay with me. I would say I maintained a pretty good balance between school, extracurriculars, and my social life. I wasn't naturally gifted when it came to tests; I was one of those guys who studied really hard but never quite got the perfect scores I was aiming for.

I was, however, some teachers' worst nightmare because, true to form, I loved to crack jokes and occasionally create chaos in the classroom. Nothing in bad taste or even close to being mean-spirited; I just loved to make a splash when I saw the opportunity. This totally depended on the teachers, of course—there were some teachers you would never disrespect because they commanded a great deal of admiration from us. I guess I acted when I saw a kink in the armor. What made things worse was that I was a goof with good grades. But, I wasn't a goof with the girls. I fell for girls and fell hard. Or, at least, I thought I did until I met Miriam.

# Chapter 8:

# First Love and Depression

When I broach the subject of girls, I always kid around with my friends that, in high school, we were riding around in Ferraris (good-looking girls), completely recklessly. You don't realize a lot of things when you're in high school; one of them is that the girls you dated had near-perfect bodies and faces. We didn't realize what we had when we were young until we got old and looked back. Life is crazy like that. I dated girls and was a loyal boyfriend. I never snuck around with other girls while I was dating.

I think the first time I fell in love was in tenth grade. Her name was Miriam and she went to a different bilingual school. I had met her in Poneloya, which is such a beautiful place to meet someone. I really do think I fell in love, although there are a lot of skeptics who would say that what I went through was more like puppy love. Well, whatever it was, it affected me tremendously.

Miriam and I dated for close to eight months. For spring break, she went on a trip to Cancun. It turned out that, on the trip, she had been with someone else. She had probably gotten drunk and met some guy. I didn't find out about this until much later, when one of her best friends had gotten into a fight with her and swore her revenge by telling me what had happened. I confronted Miriam, but she would never confess. It took me months of investigation to find out the truth. When I finally found out what she had done, I actually felt my heart break. I fell into a spell, a deep chasm of sadness and despair. I even remember waking up in the middle of the night to find out that my dream with Miriam was just a dream. *Miriam was gone.*

I had fallen so in love with her that I knew I was too mentally weak for us to stay friends. So, I decided I had to stop talking to her, and that's what I did. I vividly remember on one occasion, in front of the school, when I was just sitting there, and she came over to me. She sat next to me, and I wouldn't talk or even look her way. What I did was so hard because I was still in love with her. It shook me to the core.

I never thought someone else could affect me this much. I was torn to pieces like a million jellyfish racing upward to the surface for a last gasp of air. I was destroyed, like Humpty Dumpty without all the king's horses and all the king's men—just smashed to pieces because of what I considered to be a huge betrayal. There was no turning back. I would suffer this in silence, alone, and in the shadow of a beautiful relationship that was but could never be again.

I had to move on, but this was especially difficult when Miriam's family decided to transfer her to my school. I was a year above her, a junior, when she got there. It made my stomach do summersaults every time I saw her. It was bad. I couldn't get over her that easily, but I felt I had a chance to, at least, not have her in my classes because of the grade difference. This ended up being untrue, as we wound up having a Spanish class together. I don't understand why I didn't just go to the counselor's office to ask for a schedule change. I was in a morbid state. I couldn't let go of Miriam all the way, and even though I didn't talk to her, she would still haunt my dreams for many years to come.

Miriam had shown me what true sadness felt like. I had gone through a spectrum of emotions when it came to that particular relationship. I'd learned what it felt like to lose something that is truly dear to you. Even if I could have forgiven her, the trust was gone. With that, the magic had withered away like an old tree that was gently approaching its death, half-dead, the other half fungus and decay. I had no way out. I had to get over my loss and move on. Miriam had caused a feeling of defining sadness and remorse, but I had never considered it a depression.

To this day, I don't know if Miriam was the reason I fell into a deep depression. It didn't happen in sequence, at least. I mean, yeah, I was sad when things ended, but it didn't roll over into a depression, which happened on its own. At least, that's how I experienced it. For anyone who has ever felt depression, you know what I mean when I say that you sometimes don't know where it's coming from. Well, I can say with certainty that I believed I was completely over Miriam, but who knows; maybe in my mind I was, but my heart was still frozen in time.

Depression is no joke. For me, it meant staring at the ceiling for days on end. There was a poster in my room that my older brother, William, had left behind. It was a gorgeous woman with an almost Native American–meets-modern-world-type of look. The poster was of Mardi Gras; I can't remember the year. I just felt like life had no meaning. Looking at her was such a juxtaposition to how I felt that it was like emotional irony.

There were days that I missed school. My depression started during the summer between my junior and senior years. I was working at a bank, doing a summer internship. The funny thing about it is that I had no idea that, in Nicaragua, banks work on Saturdays. I had just messed up my summer. Why didn't I get a normal job that was from Monday to Friday? I blew it. Going on Saturdays was the biggest waste of time. I would show up with huge hangovers from the night before only to sit there from 8:00 a.m. until noon and do absolutely jack-diddly squat.

# Chapter 9:

# Thoughts of Suicide

Depression is one of the most difficult conditions to explain to another human being who has never experienced it. I had a slew of family members—from uncles to cousins to my closest friends—come and try to coax me out of my funk, as if it was even possible. I had an aunt, my father's sister, show up with cassettes of Norman Vincent Peale and *The Power of Positive Thinking*. I put it in my cassette player because I had nothing to do and nothing to lose. Nothing helped.

It got to a point where I was losing my will to live. Suicide slowly crept into my thoughts. Often, when your depression is serious, you consider suicide as the answer—the only way out of it. I can't believe how far removed I was from my true reality. For me to even consider suicide today would be impossible. Now, I know what depression is and what it feels like, so it's easy for me to go to the doctor and say, "Hey, man, I'm not feeling good. What can you do for me?" But, I couldn't do that then.

I was diagnosed with a serious depression. It's important to point out that I was a "fortunate" depressed person because I didn't have a drug or alcohol abuse problem on top of it. The two usually go hand-in-hand. To this day, when I walk into a new doctor's office and they ask me about drinking, I say, "Yeah, I drink, but not to get drunk." They all react the same way: "This kid is lying."

I was lucky that I got my depression when I did because it coincided with a cocaine epidemic that rocked some of my friends from school. I think I'm one of the only ones among them who's still never touched or tried coke. I never got past smoking weed, and even with weed, I never purchased it. I would only smoke marijuana when it was around and in the right setting—doing it with people I knew, like at someone's beach house. I didn't get high to go to concerts or parties, much less to go to class. I always thought that was kind of ridiculous, people who got high every day. What a waste.

But, suicide is no joke. By this time, we were in our second home in Managua, which coincidentally was kitty-corner from a pair of massive water tanks and next door to Bianca Jagger's pad. I shared a bathroom with my younger sister. Originally, my parents' plan was for her to have her own bathroom. The problem was that the bedroom was the one farthest from my parents' bedroom. My sister, who was only 11 at the time, pleaded to be in the room that was next to theirs. So, in the end, we ended up as almost roommates, if it hadn't been for the bathroom in between us.

Tylenol, I would overdose on that. I had already made up my mind. My parents kept this huge jar of Tylenol, and I was going to down the whole bottle. I don't remember how many I took, but Catalina witnessed the whole thing. That's something that I'll never forgive myself for. I was like Superman to her and, here I was, trying to take my life in front of her.

She scrambled for help. All I remember was a doctor coming to me with a bunch of cups of salt water. Apparently, saltwater makes you throw up. I had no idea. So, with the doctor's help, I coughed up what seemed like a never-ending stream of white pills. They came out of my mouth and even out my nose. I felt a stinging feeling inside me, like I had just been flipped inside out and all my organs were on display for everyone to see. If you can believe it, this would not be my last attempt. I tried again sometime later by overdosing on Valium. The pills must have expired because I never felt anything. I just took a nap and woke up in the same state.

With depression, you don't want to talk to or see anyone. You wake up only to look forward to going back to sleep. It's weird because, deep inside, you think that if you go to sleep, tomorrow will be a better day—but it never is. When you're depressed, everything is a mission. Personal hygiene goes out the window. I spent, probably, days or weeks at a time without showering. My face was full of acne and my hair was greasy and full of dandruff. I was disgusting. There was no way I was going to school, so education became something I did on and off. I mean, I didn't give up on it altogether; there were days that I would go, but it was painful. I was taking meds but eating very little food, so there were times I would get up and feel close to fainting, though it never happened.

During my whole struggle, I actually had a girlfriend, Martha, who was with me before I fell into that extreme depression. She was mature and sweet, and she didn't give up on me. But, I had nothing to offer. I hardly spoke and, physically, I was completely out of whack. I mean, it was normal for a kid in high school to masturbate or have sex with his girlfriend. I couldn't do any of those things. I don't know how or why she stayed with me. I really had nothing to offer. She was loyal, though, and she knew I was a good guy. I was tormented by the fact that any day she was going to break up with me.

There was one day that the meds I took caused a strange reaction in me. They made my neck get stuck in a bent position. It was quite embarrassing when it happened. It was becoming clear to me that the solution to my problem was not going to be found in Nicaragua. Because Nicaragua was kind of a new country, it was really unsophisticated when it came to a lot of things; and medicine was definitely up there on the top of the list. I mean, I endured more than three months of torture, and no one had a clue what was wrong with me.

**Chapter 10:**

# The Costa Rican Antidote

It was then that I began begging my parents to take me to Costa Rica. It was right next door and had a reputation for advanced medicine. My uncle, who was married to my father's first cousin, Rosario, had said from the beginning that I was bipolar. He was also bipolar, so I guess it's like that old saying, "It takes one to know one."

Uncle Tomaso was of Italian origin and a very good friend of my parents. We stayed at his hotel, El Balmoral, which was located right in the center of San Jose, Costa Rica's capital. The hotel was actually Aunt Rosario's inheritance from my grandfather's brother. My parents made sure we got a room on one of the lower levels. They didn't want to take any chances. The next day, we went to see the new psychiatrist.

Before moving forward with this story, I want to talk about something that most people don't understand. When you are severely depressed, the smallest things can seem like insurmountable tasks. I mention this because, during the time I was depressed, which was about three months but felt like three years, I often did not shower and sometimes didn't eat. Even a task as trivial as getting out of bed became a titanic feat. When you feel that low, you have no energy and feel like you've lost all intelligence, have no self-worth, and are a burden to others.

I mention this now because we were staying in the center of the city, and the doctor's office was within walking distance from our hotel. My mother, who had suffered greatly from all I had gone through, set the appointment for 8:00 a.m. In her mind, the earlier the better. She didn't consider the difficulty I had waking up, much less walking, at the time. It might have been that I was on the wrong meds, but whatever the reason, waking up early was a huge ordeal.

I still remember the feeling of walking to the appointment like a mummy. In the mornings, the meds made everything gray. I awoke with no initiative whatsoever. Everything was so negative that I felt like staying in bed in the fetal position was the only way to feel somewhat better. The grays would fade away as the day went by, but I still had a gloomy depression looming over me like a dark cloud.

Sometimes, I wish there were a pill that could be made to emulate depression so people who don't understand can get a taste of what a depressed person goes through. I guess it's not unlike women wanting men to understand what childbirth feels like. I'm not saying that these two things are the same; that would be crazy. The problem with clinical depression is not so much how bad you feel; it's that it doesn't allow you to see a light at the end of the tunnel.

Here's a good example: You decide to go eat ice cream with a friend and, without realizing it, you eat too fast and wind up with a brain freeze. Now, a brain freeze sucks. We've all had it and we're all glad that it's a feeling that goes away in a matter of seconds. Now, imagine a brain freeze that lingers and simply won't go away, with absolutely no end in sight. This is what makes depression extremely dangerous. The person who is depressed can't perceive an end in sight. The danger is the time passing without a cure as thoughts of suicide begin to grow.

By the time I got to Costa Rica, I had already tried to kill myself twice. Looking back now, I can't understand how I logically made that decision. But, I had one thing going for me, which is the reason I'm alive and writing this book today: I had extremely strong support from my family. My parents were never the type to minimize what I was going through. They never said, "Walk it off," "It's all in your head," or "Why are you so weak?" Another thing that saved me from myself was that my father didn't believe in guns. Having access to a gun and being bipolar is not a good combination. God only knows what would have happened if we'd owned any type of weapon like that.

At 7:00 a.m. the morning of my appointment, my mom had the fun job of trying to wake me up. I felt like I weighed a ton of bricks. I had no intention of getting up. I didn't care that I had a doctor's appointment. All I could think was *Fuck off.* I finally negotiated for 15 more minutes of sleep. I begged for it. Finally, I got out of bed. I can't even remember if I showered. I probably didn't.

So, we ate breakfast and walked over to Dr. Gallegos's office. He came highly recommended by various people. He was round and had a happy face and soft hands. He felt a little like a grandpa figure. I liked him right away. Granted, I had seen, up to this point, at least five different doctors before him in Nicaragua. This one drew me in.

Dr. Gallego had very positive energy and felt to me like a jolly spirit. *Maybe there is a cure*, I thought to myself. My mother spoke first. She described everything we had gone through. She talked about how I was a normal kid: I had always had good grades, played sports, and even had girlfriends. I was a totally normal dude until around the summer between 10th and 11th grade.

I don't remember speaking very much during my first encounter with Dr. Gallegos. He muttered some words, which I hardly understood at first. He said, "Campo—this is your last name, correct?"

I said, "Yes my last name is Campo."

He took me aside, leaving my mom in the room and taking me to another. "Hey, I want you to look inside this file cabinet." So, I did. "I want you to see how many close and maybe not-so-close relatives of yours have been through this office."

The moment he showed me this, I was struck with a feeling that was more than just a glimmer of hope and more than just a light at the end of the tunnel. This was becoming real for me. All these names had suffered something similar to what I was going through. And, once again, I felt like an alien who had finally landed on his home planet.

"It's likely, due to the fact that this particular family has a lot of bipolars, and that this is a genetic condition, that your son is bipolar," stated the doctor. My mother felt something similar to what I felt: hope. "We are going to start him off with two doses of lithium per day, one with breakfast and one with dinner. He has to try and eat normal amounts of food because the lithium can be very heavy on his stomach. In the beginning, it will be normal to have diarrhea and shaky hands as we figure out the right dose for him."

And, so my treatment began.

Chapter 11:

# And, on the Third Day, I Rose

# Again

The following things I'm going to say are hard to believe. I took the lithium like clockwork; of course, my mom saw to it that I followed the guidelines to a T. Within three days, I was out of my depression and feeling great. I will never forget the feeling. It was like Lazarus from the Bible—or even Jesus—because on the third day, I rose again.

I had a bit of madness in me from all the excitement of being back to normal. At one point, I took a lighter and let it burn for a minute. I then branded myself on the inside of my left hand where my hand meets my arm with the lighter, right on my wrist. It was insane, but it was something that somehow felt right, like leaving behind a reminder that there's always a way out. My mom was terrified when she saw it, but overall, she was happy to have her son back in good health.

We stayed in Costa Rica for a few more days as I adjusted to the meds. They did give me stomach problems—I had diarrhea for weeks. I also had shaky hands, which was extremely annoying when I got back to school because everyone could tell that I was trembling. All in all, the side effects could have been much worse. I learned to live with both.

Before starting meds, I could only go to the bathroom at home. But once this all happened, I became an international pooper. I could poop anywhere. One of my most infamous pooping experiences was in an outhouse at my uncle's farm. It was disgusting, but I played it cool, did my business, and then cleaned up with a newspaper. It was nasty but also an interesting experience at the same time.

So, there I was with a label on my forehead. It's weird, but like any normal human being, you feel relief knowing that you have something, and that you belong to a host of individuals who are going or have gone through the same experience. I was happy to know I belonged somewhere. Neither my parents nor I understood what being bipolar meant. We hadn't seen or experimented with the other side of the moon. Like Pink Floyd, the dark side of the moon was something doctors explained, but what did they know? They weren't astronauts with hands-on experience in outer space.

They tried explaining manic depression to me, but they really didn't know how. The only way to kind of glimpse at the dark side (which is actually not dark at all but instead full of euphoria) was if I happened to meet a psychiatrist who also was bipolar. This was an unlikely combination, considering how many years of study you need plus the overall stability that is also paramount in taking on a difficult profession like psychiatry. But, there were a few.

So, by the second semester of my junior year, I was back to my old self. It was as if the shackles had been taken from my feet and arms. I had a lot of things to do, which included applying to college. I saw this as an enormous monster, breathing flames of anxiety on my head. There was no way I was going to college. Too many ligaments in my brain had been torn from a well-defined clinical depression. In all honesty, I didn't believe in myself anymore.

The new me came along with lots of self-doubt, which paralyzed me when it was my turn to unsheathe the sword and slay the monster. I applied to colleges with my mother's help. She was the most understanding when it came to the academic shortcomings this new condition had provoked.

A funny side story that I want to mention has to do with lithium. Most people think that we humans naturally contain large amounts of lithium in our bodies and, because of that, we are stable. While there are mentions of lithium as naturally occurring in certain water sources, it's not in large quantities. People usually assume, "Oh, Josh has a lithium deficiency, that makes sense." This could not be further from the truth.

We don't have large quantities of lithium inside us. Doctors use lithium because, in certain quantities, it creates a more stable environment (fewer ups and downs). Lithium is a metal that looks like salt; you will see it on the periodic table. It is a drug that must be closely monitored because it can cause irreparable damage to your kidneys.

The funny part about all this was going to the doctor one day with my mother. She actually asked the doctor if he could check to see her levels of lithium. It was hilarious—both the doctor and I cracked up at my mother's ignorant yet funny question. I don't understand how people are so clueless when it comes to mental health. I made the mistake of being open about my condition in Nicaragua, a tiny country where almost everyone knows everyone else.

I've been branded all sorts of things, from crazy to who knows what. Dating, for example, has become a nightmare. Things start out well, but then I either get too excited (and go into hypomania or full-blown mania and lose my marbles) or someone tells the girl that she's dating a maniac. They say all types of things that are mostly untrue. You see, a well-balanced bipolar, one who takes his meds, doesn't do drugs (not sure if marijuana is considered a drug, but I personally have had a bad experience with it), drink like an alcoholic, and is no different from anyone else. Drugs and alcohol come with the territory for most people diagnosed with bipolar condition. You will start to realize that as we delve deeper into this memoir.

In my last months as a senior in high school, I received a beautiful gift from my godfather's wife. Her name is Carmen, and she was always very kind to me. Aunt Carmen had spent several years working at American Airlines. I'm guessing the company allows you to fly for free for years, even after you no longer work there. She gave me a gift I never expected. She told me I could go anywhere in the world as long as an American Airline flew there.

At the time, my oldest brother, William, was studying abroad at the University of Tokyo, mostly to learn Japanese. This was a once-in-a-lifetime opportunity to experience a whole other culture with my own personal tour guide. I couldn't say no to this adventure.

# Chapter 12:

# William the Overachiever

A little background on my older brother, William. William was named after my father and grandfather, essentially making him William III. Obviously, he never used this title—after all, we weren't in 16th-century England. Naming their kids after themselves was a very macho, Latino thing to do, and I hated it. These double, triple name associations only caused confusion.

When someone would call and ask for William, it was simply annoying to have to ask, "Which one, William papa o William *hijo*?" I don't think my brother ever cared that he was named after someone else because the name came with hidden perks for him. He somehow figured out a way to use my father's frequent flier miles, and boy, could my brother fly. He loved learning about different cultures. He amassed an impressive collection of *National Geographic*s. I especially remember the covers of some volumes. One was the Mayan mask of Jade, which I got to see in person when I went to my cousin's wedding in Antigua, Guatemala. The other edition of *National Geographic* that struck me was a very famous photo of an Afghan girl with piercing green eyes, covered by a burgundy cloth.

In all honesty, I don't know how many miles he was able to snipe from my father, but my brother was both stealthy and smart as a whip, and I'm certain he found an opportunity to travel for free here and there.

My brother was four years older than me. It was not too far in age, but far enough that our relationship truly blossomed when he was in college and I was in high school. William was an overachiever, to say the least. He was at the top of his class (not number one, but close) academically and strangely devoted to an ancient instrument called the French horn. Most people don't know anything about what a horn is in the same way they don't know that Africa is a continent and not a country. I was always surprised by how ignorant people can be.

The horn has been around since the 1700s and makes a very important sound needed in most classical pieces. If you've never seen a French horn, it looks like a trumpet with four keys that have been stretched ten times over and woven into intricate loops like a brass orgy, all culminating in a tiny mouthpiece and a flared bell—similar to a big, round trumpet. It's popular as a Christmas tree ornament in miniaturized form.

By correctly vibrating your lips into it while manipulating the keys with one hand and adjusting your other hand inside the bell of the instrument, you could produce all the musical notes and decide the power of the sound. It was an instrument you would see in a high-school concert band or the great symphony orchestras like Boston and New York. This was not an instrument you would ever see in a jazz or rock band, for example.

When I was a kid at home, it was commonplace to hear Bach, Mozart, Beethoven, Chopin, and Debussy. My father was a pianist and guitarist who could play some things by ear. Since he couldn't actually read music well, we basically heard the ten classics he knew over and over, along with the occasional "Happy Birthday," which he would play in the morning on his guitar to rouse the birthday kid out of bed. The whole family would show up and sing, accompanied by his guitar. It was such a beautiful tradition. It gives me chills and a sudden warmth just thinking about it.

My brother's fascination with music and diverse cultures spilled over to learning new languages like Portuguese, Italian, and Japanese. With his base languages being Spanish and English, he was fluent in five languages at one point in his life. He had an amazing self-discovery when it came to knowing so many languages. He felt that a person being able to express himself in every language offered them different personalities. This was something that fascinated him and kept him going on his journey to becoming a polyglot.

In the process of learning Japanese at his alma mater, the University of Michigan in Ann Arbor, he was accepted into an exchange program at the most prestigious university in Japan, a country of over 124 million people. (In Tokyo alone, there were 14 million people.) Japan is also the densest country on the planet. My brother went to school in the

'90s, a time when the US looked up to Japan and applauded its innovative spirit and gumption. My brother seized the great opportunity and was granted a full scholarship. It was a yearlong comprehensive program that would value both academics and cultural immersion.

# Chapter 13:

# Tune in Tokyo

It was the summer of 1997, and I was on my way to Narita International Airport in Tokyo. The day before my departure, I hung out with friends, drank lots of alcohol, and came home, where I hardly slept.

The route was Managua to Miami to Dallas/Fort Worth to Tokyo. I think the journey in total was about 20 hours long, maybe 24 hours, if you were counting layovers. From my window, I witnessed the most beautiful volcanic formations in what seemed like an endless sunset. The colors illuminated the plane with overlapping hues of orange and pink glowing, almost pulsating. It was reminiscent of the short wave of light you see just before and after sunset. On the plane, I had a whole row to myself, which made it easy for me to turn my spot into a bed. But, who was I kidding? I was so excited to see Tokyo and to see my brother, there was no way I was going to sleep.

I arrived at around 7:00 a.m. I felt strange but not really tired or even irritated. What I felt was little more than a bit of a hangover from my "bon voyage hangout night" the day before. I arrived at customs and was greeted by a jolly Japanese official who was all smiles. He saw my Nicaraguan passport and immediately greeted me in Spanish. Culture shock number one. The Japanese are highly educated people. In my mind, the chances of a Japanese official speaking Spanish were like those of a French guy speaking Russian. It was all too strange, but I embraced the situation with joy. To this day, it remains one of my favorite arrivals into a country. Such warm welcomes at airports are becoming more and more rare.

I made it through all the checkpoints and was greeted by my brother. We gave each other a long hug and even kissed each other on the cheek. "Little brother, welcome to Japan." I had finally made it across the globe to see my next of kin.

That day, we played it cool and just kinda chilled on the University of Tokyo's campus. I was surprised to see that I was much taller than just about every Japanese person. The Japanese gaze at you as if you're a movie star, which was something I took zero advantage of when meeting Japanese girls. I do have to say that I was flabbergasted by the size of my brother's living quarters. University dorms were so small; I didn't know if I was in shock or awe.

The bathroom was something that I had never encountered in my life. It was a shower combined with an American-style toilet, and it would get soaked when you showered. You had to cover the toilet paper while taking a shower. I messed that up pretty badly. My first shower was a catastrophic affair, leaving in its wake a puffed and completely soaked fresh roll of toilet paper. *What a disaster.*

In Japan, I learned a lot about a culture that is much more advanced than what I was used to. This was true, even when comparing it with American culture. These guys had it down in so many ways. Taking my first dump in a public place was such a crazy experience. William and I were at, what seemed to be, an upscale restaurant for a guy living off a language scholarship—but little did I know, he actually made bank as a language tutor at a conversation school.

The bathroom at this restaurant was a hole in the floor and two bars about a foot and a half in height, and maybe a foot in length. It was a very simple transaction: All you had to do was pull down your pants, grab the bar, crouch, and let the good times roll. It was a piece of cake and probably the cleanest shit I've ever taken in my life. That was one of my first observations of Japanese superiority. Another was that they didn't shake hands to say hello; instead, they bowed their heads slightly.

Fast-forward to Covid times in 2020, and this aversion to touch meant the Japanese were already ahead of most of the rest of the world. These guys really aren't into human contact. I saw this for the first time when my brother and I were late for some social event taking place close to the university. We had to grab the rush-hour subway, or *chikatetsu* in Japanese. Trains in Japan never run late. If the schedule said the train was arriving at 1:07 p.m., then it was arriving at 1:07 p.m., possibly earlier. Tardy trains were regularly featured on national newscasts. Name and shame.

The subway experience was such a testament to Japanese manners and culture. If the train was full, this guy with white gloves and a crisp uniform would push people into the train until it was jam-packed. Having spent a summer in New York, also while visiting my brother, I wondered why people didn't just fend for themselves. William explained that the Japanese weren't aggressive by nature, and so it was frowned upon for individuals to push one another out of the way.

On a single train car, you find three things: bars and rails to hold on to and blue and red chairs. Red chairs were reserved for the elderly, handicapped, or pregnant women. I made the mistake of seeing an empty red chair and deciding to sit in one. My brother grabbed me immediately and reprimanded me for this gesture. I wasn't at fault because I didn't understand why I couldn't sit there if no one was using them.

"This is their culture, Joshua," William explained. "And, when in Rome, do as the Romans do."

Tokyo was full of crazy, weird experiences. My brother skipped some classes to show me around. We met up with one of his girlfriends, who was visiting from Australia, and took a train trip with her to see some incredible temples full of art in a dark forest a few hours away. The place was called Nikko.

The temples and pavilions were colorful and bright, but the site in a grove of tall trees that must have been ancient gave them a sort of mystic quality. It may have been here that I felt all the excitement of the trip start to affect the way I was thinking and feeling. On the way back, I lost myself listening to my music on the train. The Beatles felt oddly mesmerizing. I felt like I was on some sort of trip. Well, I was. And, gazing out at the tiny, gray houses with their curvy deep-blue tiled roofs as the train sped by was putting me in a sublime trance.

After a few more days of sightseeing—including a gory war museum where we got to see not only the famous kamikaze airplanes we'd always heard about from World War II but also kamikaze boats and even kamikaze human bombs—I was in a serious daze and experiencing a dose of unusual excitement. The throngs on the trains and the strange food were a bit of a challenge.

I found myself having a hard time getting any shuteye in my brother's tiny rabbit-hutch dorm room, even though he decamped to his girlfriend's room nightly to leave me his bed all to myself. She was a lovely Indian girl from England named Varsha. William had a crew of friends from all over who were his mates from the exchange program and lived in different buildings together in the same dorm complex. Varsha holds the distinction of altering his taste buds for life by getting him hopelessly hooked on her homemade Indian food, which was laced with the contents of a box of spices specially shipped over from Birmingham by her mother. Both she and William coincided in their craving for flavor. They found the Japanese food that was within reach of their initial meager student allowances to be lacking in the taste scale.

A group of my brother's school friends had decided to take advantage of my visit to organize a trip out to the country. We would take the bullet train up to Fukushima to spend a few days at Yoko's country house. Yoko, an International Relations major, was one of the Japanese members of the contingent. She had spent time abroad and spoke excellent English. The whole thing sounded exciting to me, a chance to escape the throngs of Tokyo and chill out in the countryside with William and his peeps. However, by this time, I was having trouble sleeping and still not quite getting over the 14-hour jet lag, which was rougher than I'd expected, so just about anything and everything was getting me riled up.

After four hours on the Shinkansen bullet train, we reached our destination, which looked like a Japanese parking lot with some nondescript gray buildings and neon signs.

She must have noticed the look of concern on my face, because Yoko immediately told us, "No, this is just the train station. We still have to drive up to the house."

A car took us into a forest and right along a shallow, crystalline creek to a row of quaint stand-alone houses in molded white concrete, with evidently no one home. Streaks of light breaking through the canopy sparkled on the walls and gave the place a surreal feel, reminding me of something out of an anime film.

I remember nothing but a good time at Yoko's pad in the woods. We enjoyed a lot of lounging around, listening to music, and a bit of drinking, all while wearing the same pair of teal Umbro shorts. It started getting odd when I noticed William and the crew were growing physically tired of my energy. Apparently, I wasn't getting much sleep either, and during the days, I would venture farther and farther into the forest.

Losing sight of me constantly in this state was going beyond driving them crazy; it was scaring them. To me, everything seemed innocent. I was in complete bliss here—barefoot and shirtless, gallivanting in some mystical forest somewhere in the middle of Japan. My brother and his friends were growing worried I would get lost, and they were getting little to no sleep, making sure I didn't disappear. I didn't speak a lick of Japanese. If I wandered off alone, finding me would not be very fun, to say the least.

# Chapter 14:

# Losing My Marbles

Over the course of that joyful visit to the countryside, William started coming to terms with his denial and sensing there was something wrong with me. He knew I had just been through a serious bout of depression. He later told me he started altering my travel plans right then and there at Yoko's. He didn't want to take a chance on me getting worse while I was over there and ending up with a hospital incident on his hands, half a world away from home and in a totally different language and culture.

Who knows what they'd want to do to me, how long I could be trapped in a hospital, or how much that would wind up costing my parents. Worst of all, I had already managed to get accepted to college at William's alma mater, the University of Michigan. It was probably by the skin of my chinny-chin-chin, considering what had happened to my grades during my stint under the covers before discovering lithium. Most of all, he later told me, he didn't want me to miss out on starting school on time. So, for him and his friends, their eureka moment at the chalet in the forest marked the beginning of the race to get *otooto* ("brother" in Japanese) Josh out of Japan as fast as possible before the shit hit the fan.

William spoke to American Airlines and rescheduled my flight, moving it forward to give him and his friends just enough time to get me back to Tokyo and put my ass on the plane. His friends didn't mind. I was exhausting them. As some of them—whom I may have been a little too aggressive toward in my state of euphoria—fell back, two stepped up who, according to my brother, became my guiding lights and guardian angels.

Lee from Korea and Michaela from Australia took charge and were there, firmly on my butt, to get me dressed, packed, and in the car for the bullet train. We made it back to Tokyo without incident, although the Shinkansen was packed and we had to stand for four hours—who knew they oversold bullet trains? Anyway, that was probably a gift, as it sapped my energy enough to keep me still on the train.

The next leg on the commuter train to reach the dorm was another matter. I was combative with the guys and acted out on the train, frightening not only them but also the nice Japanese peeps crowded all around us in the evening rush hour. When we finally reached our station, I decided I'd had enough of being bossed around by William, Lee, and Michaela. I clutched a rail on the inside of the train and refused to disembark. I felt like Jim Morrison from the Doors. I became a rebel without a cause.

The song, *Break on Through*, repeated itself in my mind. It was one of my favorites of Jim's creations. In my mind, I felt like a rock star with a dash of feeling somewhat like Jesus. My psychosis was that I was being hunted down and that I had to escape. By the time my brother's friends noticed I wasn't interested in joining them, they were already on the platform and the doors were shut. I smiled and waved goodbye.

As the dark-orange car of the *Chuo-sen* revved up to speed, it dawned on me that I was all alone, on a random train, at night, in the middle of the world's largest city without the slightest clue as to where I was or where I was heading. Or, how to get home. Or, how to ask how to get home. Or, where home even was.

As the chill rolled down my spine, I felt someone grab my shoulder. My brother had stayed behind on his own to get me off that train. He was crying with fright and didn't say a word. The announcement came on in warbled Japanese and the train screeched to a halt.

"Joshua, you have to get off this train with me now," William said calmly. "You can't keep going. It's dangerous." And, somehow, perhaps it was the chill or the icy calm in his voice, I obeyed. William hailed a hideously expensive taxicab, and we finally made it back to the dorms, where the others were waiting.

Up in the rabbit hutch, I took up William's offer to shower, and don't know how I got confused and wound up flooding half the room. When my brother returned, the mess I left was the least of his concerns. He couldn't find me. Apparently, I got bored in the wet room and decided to go for a night stroll in the neighborhood. William couldn't believe it. After what he'd been through to get me off the train and not lose sight of me, he'd lost me straight out of his own room!

Without sparing a second, he hauled ass, running all over the dorms, yelling my name, and gathering the crew to see if anyone had seen me. His friends organized in teams to scope out different parts of the neighborhood where I might have headed, some on foot, some on bikes. My brother was praying that I didn't pull some stupid move that would get me noticed by the police and taken in. The odds were high: A foreigner at night is always a prime target for police interrogation. They mean no harm, but you're different, and they naturally want to know if that bike is really yours, what you're up to, and what you're rambling about at night.

If the police retained me, I would most likely wind up in a hospital, if I was lucky, or in jail, if I wasn't. Either way, my departure from Japan would be delayed indefinitely and become excruciatingly complicated. William and the crew were keenly aware of this. Worried as hell, they split up and acted fast.

And, me? I remembered the convenience store we'd gone to near the dorms when I first arrived and had gone down there to get—I don't know what, or just get away from the mess I'd made. I don't remember. What I do remember is one of my brother's mates, a girl from California assigned to scout the store, turned up, befriended me with candy, cigarettes, chit-chat, and a manga magazine, and convinced me to go back to the dorms with her for a smoke.

As I arrived, my brother was just getting off the phone. William and his girlfriend had cleaned up the flood. He confessed to me later that he was on the phone with my mom to let her know I would be coming home earlier than planned and lying through his teeth, denying there was anything wrong and hoping against all hopes that I would miraculously improve by merely crossing the ocean. While on the other end of the call, my mom was already in full 007 conjecture mode, being her usual worried self.

By this point, my brother—and all his friends—had acquired a singular, laser focus: They would stop at nothing to see to it that I got on that flight the next day. But between them and the goal stood one last night of keeping me under control and a painful three-hour trip through the center of Tokyo all the way to the airport, not to mention whatever shenanigans they'd have to pull to sucker the airline into letting me board a flight in this condition. They weren't about to take their chances putting me anywhere near a crowded train again. *No, sir.* We would drive all the way, preferably without stopping and with the doors securely locked with child restraints. Lee, who had experience of left-handed driving in Japan and access to requisite credit, graciously volunteered to rent a car and drive us out to Narita.

After my lost-and-found incident, the guys took turns keeping me under strict surveillance. I was not to be let out of their sight. There were always two people in the room with me that night on shifts, but I never slept—and neither did they. Next thing I knew, my bag was packed, the sun was up, and I was off on another sightseeing trip—this time to Mount Fuji, or so they told me.

I was totally stoked that we were going by car, but only William, Lee, Michaela, and Varsha were along for the ride this time. Three hours later and with still no volcano in sight, an airport popped up seemingly out of nowhere. I don't know how it never hit me that there was no trip to Mount Fuji and that I was skipping town 10 days earlier than planned. This wasn't like the train, though. I never resisted.

My brother and the two girls walked me over to the American Airlines counter to get me checked in for my flight back home. It was a long trip that, just like the inbound trip, connected through Dallas and Miami. I was so tired at this point that my energy levels were close to normal. I was being cooperative and docile, to the relief of my security detail.

William was still worried I would start acting up once I got past security and was out of their control, so he got the bright idea to register me as a child traveler, ensuring that I was supervised throughout the entire trip. I was still only 18. They handed him a small cardboard form to fill out with my name and travel details, and placed it in a transparent plastic tag that looked sort of like a baby bib that was hung around my neck. I looked like a total fool, but still, I didn't resist.

Lee and Varsha gave me hugs and bid farewell. My brother did the same and added to make sure not to take off the bib and to do whatever they asked me to do. It was for my own good and, besides, if I disobeyed the nice airline peeps, I might miss some leg of the trip, meaning it would take me even longer to make it back home. The last to say farewell was Michaela.

She handed me my backpack and gave me a huge koala-bear hug. But the deed was done. She had forgotten to take my cigarettes out of the backpack, and I was about to embark on a tedious 30-hour journey without the slightest inclination to get any sleep…

William told me they couldn't believe their luck when I made it past security and out of their sight. However, they knew the fun could start up again at any moment. So, they dragged their sad, tired, sleep-deprived selves up to the observation deck at Terminal 1 and collapsed into a heap of bodies on a wooden bench, within view of the tail engine on the MD-11 trijet that would deliver me to America. They dozed and waited, and waited and dozed.

It seemed like time stood still, yet the jet roared to life and took off, curving upward quickly into the light-blue sky, a silver streak gleaming brightly in the midday sun. Back in the terminal area—no commotion. Nothing untoward. Lee inquired as to whether all the passengers had boarded the flight safely. Everyone had made it. Hallelujah!

He drove the guys back to Tokyo and returned the car. The four of them had dinner together and crashed, still feeling drained and delirious about what they'd just been through but thankful it was over and that I had finally escaped Japan.

Chapter 15:

# Homeward Bound

Things got a little crazy on the plane. First and foremost, I was carrying lighters that had these Japanese *kanji* on them and were heavy iron-like butane gadgets. I was bringing them back as gifts for my high-school buddies. This was the first thing they confiscated. I didn't think it was such a big deal to have these fire-breathing dragons in my pockets.

The flight was also insufferably eternal—I even tried to light a cigarette on the plane. This did not exactly go swimmingly for me. The flight attendant chastised me pretty badly for the tobacco intrusion. Even though, oddly enough, smoking flights were still a thing back then, as William had found out to his bemusement earlier that same year on a backpacking excursion while flying through Bangkok and Manila on EgyptAir—where, to his surprise, smoking onboard was just fine but drinking alcohol was a big no-no.

Then, there was a moment of paranoia. I felt like someone was watching me. There was one person in particular—he looked American and had a long tail of hair. In my trance, I believed that he was Satan. I decided to go to the bathroom on the other side of the aisle to see if I could stop him from conjuring up a spell that would ultimately crescendo into my immediate death. I went into the bathroom and slowly began to take it apart, piece by piece. I truly believed there was a camera in there.

I don't know how the flight attendant reacted to the mess I was creating, though I suspect they must've known I had a mental condition and that I was just manifesting euphoria with a dash of anxiety and paranoia. Looking back today, in the post-9/11 era, who knows what would've happened. Maybe I would've ended up locked up somewhere in a federal jail or shipped straight to the Windward Barracks at Guantanamo Bay for some waterboarding sessions.

After pulling apart the bathroom on the plane, I was not handcuffed but, instead, instructed by the flight crew to take a nap. So, I faked a long nap. There was no way I could get any sleep. This is an integral part of being bipolar. When you're high, getting back to planet Earth is hard. No sleep for a week or two is commonplace. Euphoria is like watching a movie in color with 3-D effects and surround sound when you compare it to normal life. It's a great feeling, but I don't know if it compares with any illegal drugs on the market. I thank God each day for making me the way I am. Wouldn't change it for all the gold in China.

There were a lot of blackouts while I was high on life. Euphoria is like being a three-year-old and waking up to a bunch of Christmas presents under the tree. I really have a hard time describing it to people. Is it like cocaine? I have no idea. I've never tried blow (what some of my friends call it). Is it like ecstasy or mushrooms? Also drugs I've never tried. The furthest I went was smoking weed, which was fun in college but not a drug that stuck around once I became a professional.

Euphoria is a feeling so special that I often wonder why I can't just stay high and be productive at the same time. I think this is likely impossible because, first off, you feel no desire to work when you're manic, and second, your ideas are racing so fast it's almost impossible to follow up on any of them.

Life after euphoria, however, is very difficult to deal with. If you had an amazing idea while you were in an episode, that idea would be long gone by the time you made it back to home base. That is one of the most frustrating things about this illness. You speak to God and then you lose your bearings, and you find yourself back in a normal world, which sucks.

When I finally landed in Dallas, there was a team of paramedics waiting for me. We left through an emergency exit, where they proceeded to take me on an ambulance ride straight from the airport to the nuthouse. By the time I got there, my mother had flown up and was already in Dallas, waiting for me. She was in shock. She really didn't understand what was going on. That made two of us because I was pretty shaken up and there was very little to be had in the way of explanations coming from the professional bipolar hunters. I think it was then and there that I was handcuffed to two metal rods that served as perimeters for the bed.

When we got to the psychiatric hospital, I was pleasantly surprised that the place was very neat and the people were very nice. What was not so nice was the cost per night of my stay as a patient. The nightly rate was around $1,500! I can only imagine what that would have cost in Tokyo. My mom had to think fast before things got too pricey. She made some phone calls and I soon ended up back in Costa Rica at a retreat home, up in the mountains, which was mostly for recovering addicts.

I made friends with a couple of people at the *casa de campo*, as it was called. I remember Mark, a guy who was there because of addiction issues. He asked me straight-up how many times I had done heroin. That moment made me realize that I was completely in the wrong place. I also had a nurse assigned to me 24/7. He was a big, mestizo guy who was very clean-cut.

He probably weighed 300 pounds but this guy was great. He was patient and very compassionate. However, some sort of fight took place between us that I can't remember. It was violent enough to get me kicked out of the country house. Now, we were shit out of luck and my poor mother had to figure out what to do with me.

Chapter 16:

# Looking for a New Home

Now, just a bit of background with regard to Costa Rican versus Nicaraguan medicine. The difference is abysmal. Costa Rica is and has been a stable democratic country with an emphasis on educating its population for a few generations. Nicaragua, on the other hand, lost a lot of its best and brightest doctors during the great exodus that took place during the revolution and civil war in the 1980s. Costa Rica has a semi-socialist society and has far better health coverage than its neighbor to the north. Having said that, the country has public health facilities for patients who suffer from untreatable and, oftentimes, violent mental illnesses.

After the *casa de campo*, I was taken to a public mental hospital in the Pavas neighborhood of San José. I said goodbye to my mother and brothers, who were in tears. My mother couldn't believe the dilapidated mess of an institution where I was going to be hospitalized. Almost immediately, I was tied to a bed for what seemed like days. It was during my stay that Princess Diana and Mother Theresa both passed—on August 31st (Diana) and September 5th (M. Theresa). Not a lot of news about Mother Theresa surfaced; most news coverage focused on the grim circumstances surrounding the death of the Princess of Wales.

During my stay at the public psychiatric home, I spent what felt like ages tied to the bed. Different colors passed me by as I was put on a lot of heavy drugs. If you've never been tied to a bed—in a nonsexual context, of course—it's one of the worst experiences you can imagine. Certainly, one of the worst of my life.

At times, I would need to use the bathroom, but no one would listen to me. I believe that having been tied to a bed is part of the reason I don't like going on boats or getting on airplanes. Relinquishing control is often difficult for me. The isolating and powerless feeling you get from being tied to a bed for who knows how long breaks you. It's like I have a bit of post-traumatic stress disorder (PTSD).

Lucky for me, my mother came to visit every day, bringing treats like cigarettes and food. The cigarettes made me a god in a place like this, and since I was the sharing type, I gave them out to anyone who asked. I honestly preferred the friendship over the pack of smokes. I believe I spent more than a month in psychiatric rehabilitation. It was weird because I left just as I was getting used to being on the inside. I guess that's what happens to people who end up there or in prison for long terms or life sentences. But, in general, I was a happy guy.

My demeanor was never aggressive, so the orderlies got used to someone they could trust would be on good behavior. There were all sorts of people in this place. I saw a man who looked like a cross between God and Gandalf the Grey from the *Lord of the Rings* series. I was in awe.

The days went by quickly and I was slowly losing the buzz from the euphoria and coming back to planet Earth. I'm telling you; I know it's strange, but if you'd asked me then, I would have opted to stay there for the rest of my life.

Chapter 17:

# Homecoming

When I was finally released, I went home to Nicaragua. My friends were long gone, as they had all gone off to college. I felt a deep regret for having lost another academic year—first in first grade and now in my first year of college.

Lithium, however, came with some surprises, the most important one being hypothyroid syndrome, which was a secondary effect that happened to many people who took the drug. It meant my thyroid wasn't releasing enough hormones that would have, otherwise, kept my metabolism healthy. During this time, I decided to take a job with the counselor's office at my old high school. I did nothing but sleep, sleep, and sleep.

When it came to the thyroid gland, there were two predominant ways it could affect you. One was hyperthyroid, which made you hyperactive and lowered your appetite. The other was hypothyroid, which made you eat, sleep, and repeat. I started overeating, sometimes consuming 15 pancakes for breakfast, and blew up to over 200 lbs. My normal weight was around 170 lbs. I still have the stretch marks to show for all of that.

My self-esteem was at an all-time low. I was fat, I was slow, and I was always tired. I spent most of the days in the counselor's office sleeping standing up or hiding in one of the rooms to sleep. Mr. Fernandez, the head counselor, kind of looked the other way when he found me dozing off. He knew the hell I had been through and was very sympathetic. I also think he was gay and didn't mind having a young, moderately good-looking kid in his office. (This was just speculation on my part; I never heard anything about him having relationships with any student.)

Mr. Fernandez was a very kind person. A man who was, at one point, a priest-turned-educator, and he was very close to me. He said to me, one time, with regards to becoming a priest, which he believed was my calling: "You can run, but you can't hide, Josh." He basically ran the school, and he was my get-out-of-jail-free card. I loved him as a friend and as a mentor. Before we parted ways, he gave me a book called *Born for Love,* by Leo Buscalgia. The last I heard about him was that he passed away in the Dominican Republic. I was deeply saddened by this news.

After my semester with the counselor's office, my family decided it would be best for me to do something academic, so I started college at the American University of Managua, or UAM for short. I studied marketing because I thought it was the best option out of the choices available.

The college was relatively new—maybe five years old—and had a super-relaxed setting. As students, we could get up mid-class and smoke cigarettes. Classes were super informal, and I still had my hypothyroid problem in full effect. I slept in some classes but, overall, my tired and sleepy disposition was going away. I also wasn't scarfing down 15 pancakes for breakfast anymore.

I made a lot of friends, mostly girls I still see from time to time to this day. I have always thought that I have a good understanding of the feminine brain. I understand women far more than most guys. With my guy friends, I am limited to those who are not sports fanatics. I just can't keep up with watching so much tv on a weekly basis all for the sake of following sports. Honestly, I'd rather read a book than watch Wimbledon, for example.

I also can't stand a group of guys getting together to drink alcohol. This is very much a part of Nicaraguan culture. It's like the cowboy way. You're not a big, swinging dick unless you can hold your liquor and boast about the new girl you have on the side. These drinking circles are just so unproductive and there are no girls directly involved, so that's just not my thing. If an event is going to be guys on one side and girls on the other, I'd rather skip out and stay home.

Between my thyroid problem and sleeping in class, I didn't do much. I suspect the idea was to at least keep me busy somehow. I bombed my math class with a D+ and my grades were all pretty much mediocre in other subjects. I do admit there were some good times. By the end of the semester, I was no longer sleeping regularly during the day. The drugs for my hypothyroid condition had kicked in and I was back to normal.

The academic year ended and I really didn't have much to show for it. My parents had paid into the Florida prepaid college plan, so it was likely that I would now be shipped off to some school in Florida. The University of Florida had accepted me the year before, but they never touched base with me again. I had made the decision that I would go to FIU (Florida International University), back in my old hometown of Miami. I was already looking through the pamphlet and picking out a dorm room. And there I was, sending in my deposit, when something of a miracle transpired.

# Chapter 18:

# Go Blue!!!

An envelope from the University of Michigan showed up in the mail. The envelope was thick, so I knew it had to be good news. I opened it carefully and read the cover letter to myself. I couldn't believe it: Michigan was re-accepting me a year later. I don't know if this happened because I was legacy (my brother had gone to Michigan) or because it was their policy to give someone with an illness a second chance. I also wondered whether my brother had gotten directly involved so they'd give me another chance.

Either way, it didn't matter—I was ecstatic to have received the admissions letter. I went to the local store and bought some cigarettes to go about chain-smoking from all the excitement. Now, something I didn't know at the time was that the University of Michigan at Ann Arbor happens to be the most expensive public school in the US. I was surprised that my parents supported the idea—after all, they were going to pay for my studies. My brother had gone there and absolutely loved it. But he went on a full-ride music scholarship. Maybe they were confused and thought my tuition would also be covered.

Michigan is a top-25-ranked school in the nation and ranked in second place amongst public schools, after the University of Virginia. The campus (or campuses, really; there are three in the town) is gigantic, with more than 50,000 students all living in dorms or houses near the schools. You didn't need a car in Ann Arbor, which was a clutch. You could get to any class just by taking a brisk walk. Of course, this became more of a challenge during the winter, which in this part of the world is probably around 6–7 months long. It's not the cold that gets you; it's the lack of sun.

Though I never suffered from seasonal depression, there were definitely many who did. What always amused me was that a girl in a down jacket could look super hot, but when it came time to unwrap your present, you were dealing with a whole other person. The cold made it difficult to know what kind of shape a girl was in. The obvious solution was to take anything that came your way.

When spring finally arrived, you could feel the energy. Girls wearing skirts or shorts. Everyone's hormones bouncing around chaotically as you lay out to catch some long-awaited rays of sunshine at the leafy plaza called the Diag in the center of campus. It was there you would find the bronze "M" that was probably put there when the school was founded back in 1817. For a non–Ivy League school, it was an impressive date. Michigan had a lot of cultural flair—like Hash-Bash, when people would come out and smoke weed in public for just one day. There was also the saying that if you touched the bronze "M," you would fail your first blue book. (A blue book was a standard formatted notebook where you would write your exam essays or answers.) We were also home of the Naked Mile, which took place at the end of the year. The students would run a mile through the center of campus at midnight, wearing nothing but their birthday suits and sneakers. I chickened out. I think it had a lot to do with the cold and how I thought my unspeakables would react to it. The end of April can still be a bit frosty in Ann Arbor.

Then, there was the food. Ann Arbor had everything, from Indian to Korean to Vietnamese to Ethiopian. Wings from Mister Spots was a tradition. Everyone who lived in town was destined to eat there and at other venues, like Maize and Blue Deli, vaunted for the best sandwiches in the Midwest. My all-time favorites were Mr. Taos Chinese food and Bell's Pizza, but mostly because it closed at 3:00 a.m.

The nightlife was a bit odd. The fraternities dominated the scene and those in frats were kind of douchie. I mean, I was already 20 when I made it to college. One more year and I could legally buy alcohol. Why would I buy my friends and my access to booze by joining a fraternity? Anyhow, I loathed the culture and how the pledges were treated. The hazing at some of these fraternities was unreal and cruel. I also didn't like the way they treated girls.

Being in a frat at Michigan was like a license to be a dickhead and treat people with disdain. The thought process was kinda like "I have my family (my frat brothers), why do I need you?" The other party scene was the jock chasers. This involved the university athletics program, which probably included about 1,000 Big-10 athletes when you counted football, soccer, basketball, hockey, track and field, crew, and other minor sports. I never followed this crowd because I was never into watching sports. Sure, I played soccer through my high school years, but I never considered myself to be any good. I also played tennis, but, same story, I was also pretty average at that.

I arrived for my first year in Ann Arbor around two weeks before school started. I was so nonchalant about my new life in college that I missed some really important things. I didn't go to many of my international orientation activities, which were great places to meet people from around the world. I also failed to go to my math placement test, which was disastrous because I ended up in a more difficult math class with a teacher from Bulgaria who didn't really speak English. It was five days from the start of classes, and I didn't even know what dorm I'd be living in. Now, this was a major problem, so I went over to the housing department.

At Michigan, you were required to live in the dormitories during your freshman year. I showed up at the counter and said to the girl standing in front of me, "Hi, my name is Joshua Campo. I'm a freshman, and I don't have a dorm assigned to me." The girl almost lost her shit.

"You know school starts next week?" she asked incredulously.

"Yeah, I'm aware of that," I replied.

"Well, let me see what I can do for you." She started typing away on the computer and then kind of laughed with a smirk on her face. "God must love you; I have a vacancy in West Quad, which is like the best dorm you can get." I was really happy about that. So, for being irresponsible and not sorting out a dorm when I was supposed to, I was rewarded with the best dorm location on campus.

My years in Ann Arbor were the best years of my life. I still say I would give up all my possessions and bank accounts if I could do it all over again. Michigan is a special place. I mean, it was awesome, but it was also super-challenging. It was not all fun and games. There, you worked hard and you played hard.

The first lesson I learned is that you needed to get out of the dorms if you wanted to read or study for an exam. The dorms were always rowdy, and the place reeked of a mix of stale popcorn and feet. I would invite girls over to my dorm and they all commented on the smell. It was also the only all-guys dorm. It was a four-story building, mostly filled with sports-related students and maybe 50% normal guys. My hall was called Adams House and was one of the oldest dorms, if not *the* oldest dorm, on campus. The fact that there were no girls in the building was a huge bummer because it became more difficult to meet girls, and the first year of college usually dictated who your crew was going to be for the next three years.

My roommate was a Black cornerback for the football team. He was a redshirt, which meant that he was basically a permanent bench-warmer. His name was Leroy Simpson and we became close friends. I remember one time, very drunk, I challenged him to a wrestling match in the halls of the dorm. No contest, I was yelling "uncle!" in fewer than 10 seconds. I was no match for him. Although we weighed almost the same (somewhere around 185 pounds), he was pure lean muscle. I never saw him pick up a book or even go to a library or coffee shop to study.

Not everything was peaches and cream between us, though. Leroy was a messy guy. His whole wardrobe practically lived on the floor. When he needed to get dressed, he would just pick a shirt up off the floor, give it a whiff, and then decide whether it was clean enough for use. After freshman year, I lost touch with Leroy. I don't think he ever made it onto the football field, nor do I think he managed to graduate from Michigan. It was sad to see someone like him, who made it into a top sports program at a difficult school, waste his future away.

It's important to note that my first year of college was a complete disaster. I wasn't ready for so much responsibility, so I messed around and didn't take things seriously, academically speaking. My high school in Nicaragua didn't really prepare me for the amount of reading and studying we had to do. I was also super immature. I think my mental health set me back a bit, as well.

The bipolar condition often hinders personal growth and gets in the way of maturing into a more adult frame of mind. It soon dawned on me that I was failing my classes, so I took a W (which means "withdraw") on all of them the first semester. *What a disaster!* I don't know why I don't remember being reprimanded by my parents. If I didn't get any lip from them, I sure as hell should have. I'd just wasted a whole semester because of my lack of maturity and discipline.

Somehow, though, I was able to make a solid group of friends, which was a mix of girls and guys, by the end of the first year. The second year of college I did as most students at UM do, which is to move out of the dorms and into a house. My best friend was a guy named Matthew Powers. He was of Irish descent, and he played the part so well that we just called him "Irish" instead of "Matt" or "Matthew."

Irish was a fun-loving guy that everybody wanted to be around. He was just such positive energy, and he was smart as a whip. His family lived in Dayton, Ohio, which is pretty close to Ann Arbor. His family's house became my default setting when we had a break or other vacations. His family was classic Irish Catholic, so I felt that I fit in really well with them on vacations, like Easter Holiday. So, socially anyway, freshman year ended on a positive note.

# Chapter 19

# Sophomore Year and White Flight

During my sophomore year, I got together with Irish and 3 other guys—Mark, Chuck, and Dave—and we rented a three-bedroom townhouse. There were five of us, so everyone wanted the lone bedroom on the third floor instead of sharing a room with someone else. Today, thinking back, I don't know how I shared a bathroom with four other people without any problems.

The bathroom thing changes as you age, I think. You get older and you're willing to sacrifice fewer things. Having your own bathroom is definitely on the list of non-negotiables as the years go by. So, I don't remember what we did to figure out who was going to get the top room. I think we ended up drawing straws or something. What I do remember was that I didn't get the room. Chuck ended up getting it.

Life outside the dorms created a very big challenge with food. I ate a lot of chicken breast and lots—and, I mean, *lots*—of frozen burritos. I also ate at restaurants half the time, especially when it made no sense to go back home if my next class was close by. Ann Arbor was strange because it almost seemed impossible that so many students (50,000 and change) could live and walk to classes, restaurants, or what have you. It's also hard to believe that Ann Arbor was so gorgeous and yet only 45 minutes from Detroit.

There was a history to Detroit. It had suffered from a sort of social and economic decay unusual to a city that was once the epicenter of American Industry.

Detroit intrigued me. It had a very interesting history that ultimately led to its downfall as a city. It was called the "Motor City" because it was home to the Big Three car makers: General Motors, Ford, and Chrysler. For example, in 1910, Highland Park was a 120-acre facility for building Ford's famous Model T. At the time, it was the largest production center in the world.

At one point, the "Big Three" were responsible for 75% of all car sales worldwide. Detroit was a predominantly white city in the 1930s and '40s, with at least 90% of the city being white. Early on, Ford's high wages, along with international recruiting methods, turned the Motor City into one of the most racially and ethnically diverse places in America. Between World War II and the 1960s, the city's African American population rose exponentially, as "hundreds of thousands of Blacks were lured to the city by the promise of high-paying industrial jobs," according to Thomas J. Sugrue, professor of Sociology at the University of Pennsylvania (2014). However, by the "1940s, major manufacturing began moving out of cities to build new, more efficient plants and partly to shift production away from what became union strongholds."

By the 1950s, Detroit was the fourth-largest city in the US, with more than 1.85 million people, a sharp contrast to today's population of fewer than 650,000 people. As more Blacks moved into the city, many were excluded from White areas through violence and "red-lining," which was a way for the city to steer Black families away from White areas. Although Detroit produced the majority of the world's cars in the 1950s, "it was already experiencing dramatic de-industrialization, which strained the city's social fabric in horrific ways," wrote Kevin Boyle, professor of History at Northwestern University (2001).

The economic and social strain on those who felt disenfranchised in a self-segregated population rife with racial tension culminated in 1967's Detroit riots, which caused the death of 43 people and decimated more than 2,000 buildings in a 5-day period. Black residents attributed the cause of the riots mostly to police brutality. Although the exodus of White families had already begun by 1966, with 22,000 Whites leaving Detroit into nearby suburbs, the riots accelerated what later became known as "White flight."

After the riots, 67,000 White people left Detroit and were followed in 1968 by a further 80,000. Ultimately, the people who left Detroit were those who could afford it, which usually meant White families. According to Coleman Young, Detroit's first Black mayor, "The riot put Detroit on the fast track to economic desolation, mugging the city by making off with incalculable value in jobs, earnings taxes, corporate taxes, and retail dollars."

In 1986, Detroit was the murder capital of the US. This was fueled by a crack epidemic, which led to mass incarceration rates and high levels of crime and violence. So many people had left the city that, by 2013, the city of Detroit declared bankruptcy. To this day, you can still go into the city and witness mammoth buildings plagued with decay. These structures, which were once proud places of employment for car makers, are now only "rotting hulks of old factory buildings," filled only with memories and ghosts of the past.

All this happened a mere 45 minutes away from Ann Arbor, a calm and peaceful student town of about 120,000 people and home to the University of Michigan. All I can remember about Ann Arbor was how beautiful the campus was. The town was made up of large homes, which were perfect for its 50,000-person student body. It catered perfectly to the students, as there was a high amount of diversity in cuisine and entertainment. On any given day, you could have dinner at an authentic Indian, Ethiopian, or even Vietnamese restaurant. And, all of this was within walking distance for all the students who lived in Ann Arbor.

I started to get my shit together by my sophomore year. I was spending more time in the library and cafes to read and study and less time at home, where there were always distractions. I worked hard and played harder. I was beginning to figure out how to balance my academic and social lives.

Halloween that year was one of the greatest nights ever. I dressed up as a stripper, wearing a black tie and these yellow pants I had borrowed from my roommate, plus a white vest that was part of my tux that I had used for Glee club. The girls ate it up. I was fondled all night long by strangers' hands trying to cop a feel off this crazy Latin kid in the center of a huge school, located in the heart of America, the Midwest.

That night went down in the books as one of craziest, most fun-filled nights I ever experienced as a student in Ann Arbor. I had a conch shell that I had brought from Nicaragua and I would use it as an excuse to get girls into my room. The conch became so infamous as a successful prop to get girls into my bed that my friends would spend all the time they could poking fun at the girls who had fallen prey to the conch.

Though I aspired to be one, I really wasn't much of a ladies' man. Hooking up with girls was far different than how things were done back home. I mean, I was used to meeting a girl and then inviting her out to eat or something, but this was somehow very different. If you didn't join a frat, you would still end up at one of their parties, and the way to get girls there was simply by going up behind them and dancing. This was crazy to witness at first. I wasn't used to such a simple way of hooking up. I kind of shied away from this method, at first, but I definitely had more game as I got older. By junior year, I felt more secure with myself.

I passed all my classes my sophomore year but got a pretty low grade in math again. However, this time, a low grade in math was excusable because it was taught by a Croatian graduate student. His English was impossible to understand. It was a mission to get through every class. I attribute my bad grades there to communication issues. And even though I got a bad grade, I managed to pass the class with flying colors. My grades were steadily improving, and I was also maturing into an adult who started to recognize all the sacrifices my parents were making to keep me in school.

Chapter 20:

# Junior Year Disaster

For my junior year, I made the decision to live alone in an apartment that was closer to campus and fairly inexpensive. It was the worst mistake of my whole time as a student at UM. The room was like an underground bunker. It resembled a dungeon and was located on the basement floor of an apartment building. There were windows that let in some light, but otherwise, it was basically a basement converted into a room. I lost all connection with my friends and began to fall into a mild and troubling depression.

I spent my first semester as a junior in an isolated state of despair that I, myself, could not recognize. The only reason I didn't sink too low into depression was because I was still a busy student. I was fighting to keep my grades up and make it to class every day, though, I can't lie. Sometimes, going to class early became difficult for me.

I call depression "the red-tailed dragon." Now that I'm an experienced bipolar, with more than 29 years of dealing with this disorder under my belt, I know how to recognize when I'm getting a bit down and falling into the depths of depression. My instinct today is to act fast and look for the doctor's help when I start to feel things going south. I call the state prior to getting depressed, or "seeing the red tail of the dragon." When I see the red tail, I know the dragon is near. Being conquered by the red-tailed dragon means falling into a paralyzed state of agony and sadness. You think your world is over; even easy things like waking up and showering become difficult.

I honestly don't know why I made such a stupid decision to live all by myself. I quickly learned that a lot of my mental well-being came from surrounding myself with friends and people I loved. That semester was the worst one I suffered in the entire four years I was in college. I had guests over once in a blue moon, but my living conditions were dark and gloomy. The weather in Ann Arbor didn't help, as the sky was almost always a gray haze during fall and winter.

I knew I had to get out of that apartment for my second semester of junior year, so I decided to sublet it at a higher price than what I had been paying. Since the location was so central, it was not that difficult to find a taker. I think the guy's name was John Peters. I only showed the apartment once and got him to pay me something like $150 more than what I paid.

Now, I had a bit of extra earnings every month, which was great, and John always paid on time, which was amazing. He later came to me because the apartment had some weird heating issues that cost him a lot of money. That was probably the reason the apartment was so cheap. It seemed like the apartment was paying for the heating for the whole building. I never quite understood what had happened there, but John ended up paying the bill. After all, he couldn't blame something like that on me—I didn't own the apartment.

Once I had secured a sublet contract with John, I started to look for new digs for the second half of my junior year (from January to June). I got really lucky because one of my friends was leaving to do a semester abroad in Spain. She had been living in a famous house known as the "Church on Church." It was called that because the house was literally a church that was converted into two houses located on Church Street. I had five roommates in this house, which made it loads of fun. I ended up with a pretty cool room on the second floor, which I accessed via a catwalk. It was a nice-sized room, and living with all these people was a blast for me.

My life had changed drastically from a dull dungeon to a super-fun living environment. The tail of the dragon was gone. I had two roommates, Adrienne and Ben, who smoked pot regularly at the house. I began to smoke with them at least twice a week, if not more. Marijuana is not a great drug to take if you're bipolar. First of all, it is not a controlled substance, so the potency is different every time you smoke. There are hundreds of varieties of this stuff—from pot that just made you sleepy to some that were sophisticated and would put you in a trance. All I know is that I had no business getting involved in smoking this stuff. This, coupled with the new and fun environment I was living in, spiraled into a manic episode.

I remember doing one odd thing that made it clear I was starting to lose control. I had eaten a banana and threw the peel against the window. The banana peel stuck on the window, and I made no effort to take it down. My roommates were beginning to see a change in me—I started to play loud music almost all the time. They knew of my condition, so they began to get really worried about me. It wasn't until my roommate, James, came to me that I was saved from doing more manic things in the house. James was older than me and had a very chill-like disposition. He came up and said that he thought that I should go to the doctor for a checkup because I "didn't look so well."

To this day, I have a hard time understanding how docile and agreeable I was to the idea of going to the hospital. In my mind, I was just going to prove that I was okay, but I wasn't. I was at the beginning of a full-on manic episode. With James's help, we were able to catch things before they got completely out of hand. He drove me to the University Hospital.

It was around February, at the height of winter, when temperatures could go down to almost -40 degrees with windchill. It was extremely cold, but I was kind of numb to it. Part of the manic episode granted me some superpowers that made me immune to the cold. My mania was already snowballing into me, getting full of adrenaline and serotonin. I was feeling great, and I was convinced there was nothing wrong with me, so I went to the doctor willingly.

I was almost immediately admitted to the psych ward. I imagine that one of my roommates had been in contact with my family to let them know what was going on. My father then decided that he would make the trip up to Ann Arbor all the way from Nicaragua. In the psych ward, I was given a heavy drug called haloperidol (or Haldol, for short), which is commonly used to treat schizophrenia. It has terrible side effects, including dizziness and trouble seeing straight. I knew right away that it wasn't the right medicine for me.

It got to the point that I must've done something wrong because I ended up in an isolation chamber. There, it was just a room and a bed with no covers. I was freezing to death in there, so I kept banging on the window to tell the nurse to hook me up with a blanket. She paid no attention to me, just totally ignored me. I felt like I was being treated like an animal. *Why couldn't she just ask what was wrong?* It was so cold, I couldn't take it anymore.

I tried and tried to get the nurse to come, but she wouldn't even acknowledge my existence. *What the fuck?! I'm freezing to death in here,* I thought to myself. Finally, the only thing that occurred to me was to raise my bed onto the window so that the mattress covered the whole window frame. About five minutes later, I was paid a lovely visit by three orderlies who proceeded to forcefully grab me and carry me out of the room. They then, promptly and predictably, tied me to a bed. Well, that sucked; I went from bad to worse, and I was still on this mind-numbing formula of Haldol with who knows what else.

My father finally made it to Ann Arbor. I felt so bad for him. After all, he had never experienced this kind of weather. He wasn't prepared for the arctic blast of Michigan in mid-February. I know that he froze his ass off getting to Ann Arbor, but he was willing to sacrifice anything to get his son's health back to normal. He quickly began getting involved in the meds I was being given. We knew by then that I responded well to a medicine called Clozapine when I was fully manic. Clozapine is a psychiatric medicine used to treat psychosis and was the first atypical antipsychotic to be discovered. It's commonly used to treat schizophrenia and schizoaffective disorder.

The doctors at the psych ward were hesitant to change me off Haldol and onto Clozapine, mostly because this first-generation drug could have some nasty side effects. But, as I said, we had already used this drug on my last manic episode that ended in Costa Rica. It worked very well with me, and the only side effect that I suffered was extreme constipation. My father stood his ground in getting them to change my meds to Clozapine and they finally conceded. Even with my new regimen of drugs, it took me about 20 days to get back to normal.

I admitted everything to my parents about smoking marijuana regularly and that I felt responsible for what went down. I'm certain that weed plus a new fun house, full of friends, was the trigger that caused this episode. After I was finally released from the hospital, I took the rest of the semester off, withdrew from all my classes, and went back home. I came back for summer classes because that was the only way I was going to be able to graduate on time. I had to graduate in four years because right behind me was my sister, Catalina, who was going to be starting college right as I graduated. My parents certainly couldn't afford to have us both in college at the same time.

My parents wanted to hold me accountable for what had happened because of my negligence in smoking marijuana compulsively. No one will ever know for sure if that was the reason I had the episode, but it certainly didn't help. They said I was going to be held responsible for paying the hospital bill, which ended up being close to $25,000. So, I took on the debt and scheduled a payment plan that I could afford.

I was paying a little over $200 a month, and it took me more than 10 years to pay it off. I think it was smart of my parents to do this because it made me own up to the substance abuse that did not help my condition. I hardly ever smoked weed again after that. I'd love to tell you that I quit cold turkey, but that would be a lie. Today, I wouldn't touch the stuff with a 10-foot pole, but a lot of time has passed since then.

# Chapter 21:

# Graduation and Back to the

# Tropics

In the summer of 2002, I finally graduated from the University of Michigan with a double major in Political Science and History. How I was able to pull this off in four years is nothing short of a miracle. It was bittersweet to have to leave my beloved friends and my beloved Ann Arbor. Those were the best years of my life, but now it was on to bigger and better things.

Mr. Fernandez, the same guy who had given me a job while I was in full hypothyroid daze, was now offering me a job as a high school history teacher. There weren't many options when I graduated due to the 9/11 terrorist attacks on the World Trade Center in the heart of Manhattan that had just happened. When I was graduating, even the badasses with Master's degrees from Michigan's Ross School of Business weren't getting hired.

A part of me wanted to stay, but another part said it was time to head home. I was torn. On the one hand, I could have moved to Washington, DC, and followed my calling to be a part of the U.S. government, but the other hand told me that I could better serve my people by returning to Nicaragua. It was a tough decision.

Ultimately, I decided to return to Nicaragua. After all, in a country that was so small (with a population of only 5 million people), there were many ways I could help out. While living there, my philosophy was always to help those who are close to you, maybe someone who works for you or someone you know who is going through a rough patch and needs some extra help. At first, I began helping people by loaning them money. I quickly learned that the best way to get rid of someone in your life is to loan them money. People whom you loan money to will avoid you like the bubonic plague. I mean, for loaning out $200, I lost friendships like you wouldn't believe.

I was brought up Catholic, so I'm a big believer in forgiveness. That and practicing humility are two things I try to use as my guide for everyday living. Today, if someone asks me for a big loan, I come down on the amount and tell them that I won't loan them any money, but I can give it to them as a gift. This has worked out well in keeping my relationships with friends, colleagues, or even people who work for me. Now, sometimes, I must admit, when it comes to workers who are working for minimum wage, I'm open to perhaps a larger amount to work with; but in that type of situation, I give them a loan fully expecting that they won't pay it back. I know that doing it that way, for some who are living below the poverty line, almost guarantees they won't come back to ask for more.

Money is a tough subject to deal with when you live in a country like Nicaragua. We are the second-poorest country in the Western Hemisphere right behind Haiti. There's always someone who needs financial help and, unfortunately, I'm not a millionaire, so I have to be choosy with who I can help. On the subject of giving out money and helping out people, I had an incident with a girl named Sara.

Sara and I had a one-night stand that became kind of a nightmare scenario when she called to tell me she was late and had missed her period. I know that I had used protection when we did it, but I believed her and, as a result, embarked upon a journey of manipulation and deceit. She made me believe that the baby she was carrying was mine and called to ask for money for an abortion. The thought of helping her do this only crossed my mind for a brief moment. I remember reaching out to a good friend of mine, Sergio, who was my neighbor at the time and also a devout Catholic. He graciously helped to guide me in my situation, which was starting to feel like despair.

Sara called and told me that she needed the money to get what, in my mind, was the unthinkable: an abortion. If the baby was mine, I was prepared to raise her on my own. So, she started calling me with a very bad attitude, and this started to take a toll on my mental health. On the one hand, I was thrilled that I was going to be a father; on the other, I was worried about how I was going to get along with the baby's mother for the rest of my life. So far, she was treating me like shit, and I surely didn't deserve it.

I made it clear that I wasn't about to pay for an abortion and that I would see it through that the child got all the proper medical attention so that it would be born healthy. I ended up scheduling an appointment with Dr. Sanchez, a well-known doctor whom I trusted greatly. I told Sara that I'd go with her and pay for the doctor's consultation, which I think was about $150. I think Sara saw that I was a generous, good-natured person and figured she could take advantage of me. She began to ask me for money for things that were baby-related like a carriage and a crib. When all was said and done, between the appointments with the doctors and the baby items, I had spent about $5,000, and still her attitude continued to be hostile toward me, which I couldn't understand. By this point, she had pushed me away from going to the doctor's appointments, which I thought was very strange.

At some point between the stress and euphoria of becoming a dad, I fell into a manic episode. Big changes in one's life, like becoming a new father, can easily trigger anyone who is bipolar into a state of euphoria, followed by a strong dose of psychosis. My parents were keenly aware of what was going on, so I didn't really experience a full-blown manic attack. Instead, I had what doctors call a "hypomanic episode." This is an episode where you get the euphoria, but it's caught ahead of time, so it doesn't go into a full-blown cycle of mania—which, most often, ends in a psychotic episode where reality gets bent and blurred.

Sara and Silvia (Sara had named the baby Silvia without even taking me into account) were going around in my head obsessively. The way I was being treated by Sara just didn't make sense. By this point, I had decided to give Sara an allowance to cover everything doctor-related. She continued to treat me with hostility, and I still didn't understand why.

I was calling the doctor independently to see how the baby was doing. He had told me that everything was fine, but that Sara had requested for me not to be involved. The doctor explained that if the patient didn't wish for me to be involved, then he had to abide by her wishes.

In our last phone call, he basically said, "Quit calling me. I can't give you more information, and so far, the baby is well. Everything looks good."

Things weren't adding up. This was a one-night stand and I had used protection. I started to believe I was being taken for a ride around Gullible Lane. Sara eventually disappeared, and I never heard from her again. I obviously stopped writing her checks. She finally fessed up and repeated over and over to me, "The baby's not yours."

It took me a long time to get over what had happened; I was also in awe over how someone could take advantage of me so easily. My parents consoled me and told me that the baby wasn't mine because there was no way a mother would let go of a good man who was taking care of her financially. Sara knew that I would eventually take a paternity test and find out that Silvia wasn't mine.

Some background on my family that is important to note. My brother Eduardo, who is three years older than me, was born in Costa Rica. He was born there instead of Nicaragua because the earthquake of 1972 destroyed all of the country's best medical facilities. Since my parents had the means, at that time, they decided to go to San Jose to give birth to my brother, Francisco.

Well, in the case of Francisco, doctors told my parents that he was going to have several issues and would be a disadvantaged child. Some doctors even recommended an abortion. My parents, who are Roman Catholic, would not accept this idea and were ready to go through the pregnancy no matter what lay ahead. I'm glad that they went through it all with the strength of their conviction, because today, Francisco is thriving. He has his own business of exporting exotic animals like baby imperator boa constrictors, wood turtles, red-cheeked mud turtles, red-eyed tree frogs, green basilisks, and emerald swift lizards. He has been happily married for almost 19 years and lives a healthy life. He does not drink alcohol or smoke cigarettes, activities that are par for the course in Nicaragua. You could say that drinking either rum, beer, or wine, which is deeply ingrained into our society, is part of the culture here, but my brother has never imbibed, which puts him in a very healthy category.

What's so crazy is that my family was always concerned with Francisco's future when he was younger, and he turned out to be the most successful and accomplished of all my siblings. Francisco and I have been very close since we were kids because we always shared the same room and spent a lot of time together.

Francisco is a bit introverted by nature, so it's not as easy for him to make friends. When we were growing up, he would hang out with my friends, and everybody loved him. If anyone ever tried to bully him or me, we were always there, ready to defend each other when necessary. We didn't have too many bullying problems growing up. If anything, I would get bullied more because I, sometimes, didn't know which girls already had boyfriends. I could be a bit too friendly with them, but that's a whole other story.

The last time I saw Sara was maybe three years later, randomly, at a restaurant on the beach. I saw her out of the corner of my eye. I got up immediately and said hello and gave her a big hug, which she naturally wasn't expecting. I don't hold grudges, so I wanted to show her that I wasn't upset about what she had done. I was $5,000 poorer, but no harm done. I asked about Silvia and how she was doing. She said that Silvia was good, healthy, and growing fast. It makes me feel good that I was able to at least influence Sara to not have an abortion. I'm sure that, today, she's happy that she has Silvia in her life.

One part of my life has always struck me as ironic. I'm 46 and I don't have a wife or kids. What's ironic is that I'm great with kids. I spend all my family get-togethers with my younger cousins. I'm either on the floor, playing hide-and-seek, or organizing a game of soccer with them. I love spending time with my cousins. Since my dad is the oldest of eight children, his brothers (I only have one aunt, Mariela, and her only daughter, Monica, who recently graduated from college) all have young children who aren't so young anymore. But now the kids I pay attention to are my older cousins' kids. I mean, it's a bit ironic that I'm not married with children, but it also makes sense because of all my instability. My hope is to find stability someday and, hopefully, also find a girl who has similar values to mine and maybe start a family—if it makes sense at the moment.

# Chapter 22:

# ANS Again

My love of children spilled over into my first job after college, which was teaching history at my old high school, ANS. It was easy to get the job because I had majored in History and Political Science at Michigan. That, coupled with the fact that Mr. Fernandez still called the shots, made landing the job a breeze. Mr. Fernandez, as you may recall, was the one that gave me a job when I was going through my hypothyroid crisis.

The first day of work was a week before school started. That is the norm in most schools, as teachers need time to prepare for the upcoming academic year. The first day was odd because I had to see old teachers who I had not always been so nice to. This was super awkward, at first, but I got over it rather quickly, as I asked most of them for forgiveness, and they understood that I was just young and immature when I was in high school.

On my first day, they announced that there was a vacancy in one of the subjects. It was an advanced placement (AP) class, which meant it gave college credit to those who passed a test at the end of the year. I had just graduated and must've thought I was a badass, because when they said there was an opening in AP European History, I volunteered without flinching. Little did I know that the book I would be teaching from was 1,200 pages long and covered everything from the Renaissance to the founding of the United Nations. I would have to teach almost 600 years of history while also teaching Modern U.S. History (from the Civil War to the present). It was insane that I took on this amount of work in my first year with zero teaching experience.

Teaching was one of the best jobs I've ever had. I loved my students, even though not all of them loved me back. I had to be very strict because, if you weren't, students would walk all over you. My first year was a huge challenge. Just teaching AP European History took most of my time. After all, my kids would receive a grade at the end of the AP standardized test. As a teacher, this would either make me look good or make me look bad.

I honestly hated teaching U.S. History because it seemed so boring compared to European History. I mean, Europe is interesting; you get to teach about royal families like the Hapsburgs, Romanoffs, Stuarts, and the House of Bourbon, to name a few, and all the wars and royal weddings. The pairing of royals most often represented huge real estate transactions as royal families strategically married their kids off to other royals so they could extend their landholdings while also consolidating power.

I was especially drawn to the history of Spain and how Isabela I of Castille married Ferdinand II of Aragon to unite all of Spain under one crown. This was when Cristopher Columbus came into the picture as a Genoese entrepreneur, looking to cross the Atlantic in search of a way to secure highly coveted spices from Asia. Columbus found no takers among the fragmented principalities of what was to become Italy or any support in Portugal, but was granted a voyage funded by Spain after craftily convincing the queen. This turned out to be a very profitable wager on the part of Isabela and Ferdinand, as Columbus ended up finding a whole new continent later dubbed "America." The gold that they went on to extract there made Spain a very powerful country.

That discovery, coupled with the royal wedding between Juana la Loca (Joan the Mad—a suspected fellow bipolar), the Spanish Crown's eldest daughter, and Felipe el Hermoso (Phillip the Fair), the heir to the Austrian Hapsburg family, secured a massive empire that spanned a bit more than half the European continent. Phillip and Juana's offspring was christened Carlos I, but he is better known under his Habsburg title, Holy Roman Emperor, Charles V. He was arguably the most powerful sovereign to have ever lived at that point in history. His dominions in Europe included the Holy Roman Empire, which extended from Germany to northern Italy; Austria; the Netherlands; and, most importantly, Spain, which included possessions in the southern Italian kingdoms of Naples, Sicily, and Sardinia, plus all the newly acquired colonies in the Americas. Charles V ruled over the first collection of realms labeled "the empire on which the sun never sets."

Teaching about the Robber Barons, like Carnegie and Rockefeller, in U.S. history just couldn't measure up to the excitement I felt teaching the European stuff. It wasn't as compelling. Teaching AP European History was a titanic feat. I was so young and had so much energy that I was, somehow, able to deliver. I did wake up one day with a cheek stuck to my neck, which was a muscular problem that happened when I was stressed, but other than that, I was able to pull it off. About 80% of my class passed the AP exam, which was a bona-fide sign that I had kicked ass on the job. I was very happy with the outcome and especially proud of my students who had gotten a 5, which was the best score you could get. I had maybe four students who accomplished that.

My second year of teaching was a breeze because I only had to teach one subject—tenth-grade World History. This was a year that I really enjoyed teaching because, compared with the giant workload I took on during my first year, the second year was all downhill. I learned how to make it fun for myself, as well as for my students. The first thing I did was to put a cut-out of all the continents on the back wall. This was really cool because, whenever I had a student acting out, I would tell him, "Hey, Pedro, I need you to move from Africa to Europe." I also taught while wearing slippers, which made it easy to stay on my feet all day. My students thought I was half-crazy and half-fun.

The day before an exam, I would take out a tennis ball and do a review of the chapter we had studied that week. I would launch the ball at the most unsuspecting student, and as he caught it, I would ask a question that would be on the test. I made my class easy and fun. When we reached World War I, I was able to get some MREs (Meals Ready to Eat) from my cousin, who was an Iraq War veteran. I took my students out to the forest and took out the MREs. They were stunned. I went above and beyond with these kids, and they were so much nicer than the students I'd had the year before. I felt like I had the perfect kids that year.

Those two years of teaching were very stable times for me. I hardly remembered that I was bipolar. I took my meds and went to class. How I made it to school every day at 7:00 a.m. remains a mystery to me. Today, I can hardly get up by 9:00 a.m. It just takes so many meds to get me to sleep that morning becomes a particularly difficult time. These days, I always wake up to a mild hangover with a little bit of depression thrown in for good measure. Teaching gave me a rigid structure. It's most likely that this was what my dark passenger needed, because I never experienced a single manic episode over the course of those two years as a teacher.

Sometime during the second year of teaching, I kind of realized that I was never going to be able to make a living in that profession. After all, I was supposedly getting better pay than normal teachers and my paycheck came out to less than $1,000 a month. I couldn't live off that forever, and the only way up in teaching was to become an administrator, like a principal, which didn't strike my fancy in the slightest bit.

I loved my kids and I loved teaching, but after my second year, I decided it made sense to dabble a bit in the family business of real estate. Real estate was a whole different animal, and it was a challenge to teach and sell homes at the same time. I mean, one minute I was talking about Napoleon Bonaparte and the next I was talking about the best features of a house for sale. It took a lot of effort to get my brain to be in both places at once, but you can accomplish anything you set your mind to. Teaching was great and I loved it, but there was also a great injustice going on at the school, which I became very vocal about.

At the school, there were two types of hires: a local hire and a foreign hire. The salary difference between these two was frustrating. While a local hire made maybe $1,000 a month, the foreign hires made $2,000 plus benefits like housing, health insurance, and school-funded trips to return to their respective home countries twice a year. I thought this was unfair, especially for me.

I had graduated from a top school, which was one of the most expensive public universities in the US, and many of these foreign teachers came from rinky-dink no-name universities to make twice as much as I did. I had to speak out about it, and since I had already decided that I was not going to continue teaching, I set out to help my local-hire colleagues by being their advocate. They had more to lose than I did. In other words, I became an outspoken critic for those who were forced into silence about the salary disparity for fear of losing their jobs.

The way I saw things was a job was a job. If my job was to shovel snow, and my neighbor had the same job, then we should both get paid the same for doing the same job. "Simple, honest, and fair" was my motto. This definitely rubbed the school the wrong way. I went from being a great teacher to a grave nuisance. I think they were relieved when I signed the contract stating I wouldn't be coming back for another year. After all, I was a fire-starter who already had another job lined up and decided to make some noise.

I understand that, when I left, they did end up modifying things a bit to make up for the difference. I mean, it was just silly that people like Mr. Ruiz, who had worked at the school for more than 15 years and was, on top of that, a great teacher, made less than a couple of random Canadians who came in with no teaching experience. It was unfair and needed some correction. In the end, I was happy to hear that they had improved things for local hires after my departure.

# Chapter 23:

# Family Business

Working in real estate in Nicaragua posed significant challenges. One of the biggest was that it was easy to get screwed over by a buyer or a seller. The court systems in Nicaragua are slow, and sometimes you just don't have the time to go around, suing everyone who takes advantage of you.

One case still makes me laugh inside. I was working with a guy named Juan, showing him commercial offices in the center of Managua. I showed him one he liked, so I got him to make an offer. As soon as he made the offer, I relayed it back to the listing agent, who was actually my Aunt Carmen. She was married to my dad's youngest brother and a gracious contributor of my flight to Japan many moons ago.

So, as soon as she got the offer, she sent an email to the owner of the office space and then followed up with a phone call. The owner was apparently in Mexico City on business, but they were able to talk for a bit about the offer. In the email and the phone call, first and last names were disclosed, which meant I had a formal offer in writing from the buyer. Three months later, we realized that Juan had gone directly to the owner of the space and purchased it without going through the broker—in this case, me.

We fought tooth and nail for this commission because we knew we had the smoking gun, which was the email with a clear offer that also included the full name of the buyer. The buyer turned around and said that I'd never shown him the property and I was a liar. My name was being dragged around on the floor, which is a saying in Spanish when someone slanders you. My aunt went straight to the owner and told him that we had worked with Juan and that he had gone directly to them without going through our real estate firm. The owner had claimed that I had not shown the office space to the client because Juan had given them his word that I'd never even worked with him.

I was livid by then, but I always tried to be professional, so I kept my cool. Carmen went ahead and told the owner, "Hey, how about if we have proof that we took the client to that office space?"

The owner replied, "Sure, show me your proof."

Thank God my aunt hadn't erased the offer that was made in the email. So, she re-sent the offer, which had everything we needed: time, date, name of customer, amount of the offer, and the exact location of the office space. All of this was presented, but the owner still insisted that I was a liar and had never taken Juan to the property. I couldn't believe it. We had to go as far as to speak with the owner's parents, who were dear friends of my family, to tell them what was going on. During all that time, I was being slandered left and right by people saying that I'd never gone with the client, despite having a formal offer in writing.

The ordeal took a total of about three months of fighting and holding meetings with the owner. In the end, I was paid my commission, but was still really pissed off about how they tried to ruin my reputation. Overall, I can say that real estate is a lucrative endeavor, but in Nicaragua, you're going to get screwed out of a commission at least once or twice a year, on average. It's rare to get paid once someone goes around you, so you have to be willing to continue with a positive attitude, cut your losses, forgive the people who screwed you over, and simply move on.

Nicaragua is a little bit like Japan. Though I was manic most of the time that I was there, I did pick up on some aspects of the culture. In Japan, honor is everything, so getting shamed for doing something dishonest is worse than a jail sentence. In Nicaragua, honor is important, as well; the only difference is that, in my country, a crook doesn't feel shame, even if he's called out for doing something dishonest.

It's even worse than that because society is so intimate that you almost need to pretend that you don't know about something somebody did that was dishonest. In other words, it's such a small country that you have no choice but to accept everyone, warts and all, because you'll inevitably run into that person everywhere you go. Whether it's a restaurant, bar, supermarket, the gym, or even a barber shop, you'll run into people who don't subscribe to the values of honesty and hard work. You just have to smile, extend your hand, and not judge people, even if you know they may have screwed over a friend or family member—or even you, for that matter. It never stops being challenging, but that's just life in the tropics.

During my time in real estate, which has been more than 20 years now, I've been able to grow our company from operating exclusively in Managua by opening new franchises in three other cities. Two of them, Leon and San Juan del Sur, serve the Pacific coast of Nicaragua, where there are always surfers and investors looking for a good deal on the beach. The third office is in Granada, which is a small, charming colonial town about 45 minutes from Managua, making it an ideal place to buy a home and retire.

Granada was founded by the Spanish in 1524, making it one of the oldest settlements on the American mainland. Our clients are, most often, what we call "snowbirds," who come from the US, Canada, or Europe to get away from the cold, which, for them, is from December to March. A lot of these snowbirds end up falling in love with Nicaragua. The surf here is phenomenal, and there are almost always good waves. Plus, we have more than 300 days of sunshine year-round.

The people of Nicaragua are well-known for being open and inviting. A lot of the population speaks English because many of them returned to the country in the '90s after spending about 10 years abroad during the revolution and civil war, in places like Los Angeles, Houston, and New Orleans. Miami is in its own category; I believe more Nicaraguans were living in Miami than in the other three cities I mentioned, combined. Our business in San Juan del Sur was especially lucrative from when we opened in 2004 until 2007, as people from the US and Canada were taking out home-equity loans to buy property in Nicaragua.

Our firm was doing well, and I had great business partners. One of them was a Jewish guy from Boston who fell in love with a Nicaraguan girl and wound up staying here; the other was an American from Tennessee with a strong Armenian background, who had come down with the Peace Corps and had also fallen in love with the country and stayed. The most important thing about my partners is that I can trust them with my life. We've been through so much together that, today, I trust them blindly with any and all of my affairs.

They have also been very accepting of my illness, which made things so much better for me because, when I get manic, they are understanding and know how to handle me. I want to take a moment to give thanks to my partners and their wives, and how they've taken care of me and been there for me on all those occasions when I've been manic or depressed.

Real estate is almost the perfect job for a bipolar, because if you can't handle a client, then you just refer them to someone else. I mean, it's not ideal to lose a month's worth of work, but sometimes it happens. I know that, during those times, the people who work with me all have great respect and love for me, so they are very understanding. This goes for the women in my office in Managua, where I'm the only guy working with 12 hens, including my mother.

Working with a mother or father is hardly ideal—it requires a great amount of patience. It's actually not the most recommended setup according to scholars who've broached the subject (and also according to me). I still work for the firm out of our Managua office, and our three other franchises are still alive and kicking, thankfully.

# Chapter 24:

# Tough Love

I've had great success and luck in business. Unfortunately, this hasn't been the case when it comes to intimate relationships. It's hard for me to fall in love and not wind up unwittingly relinquishing control and falling into a manic episode. Finding a girl I really like goes straight to heavy infatuation, of the sort, which I end up obsessing about.

The obsession usually trickles into a manic episode, so finding a significant other is tricky. Plus, even if I get through the infatuation and end up dating the girl, my mind will self-sabotage the relationship because I often wake up with a bit of a downer. These black mornings cause me to question everything, including who I'm dating. On average, my relationships don't last more than a year. Often, while reminiscing, I say to myself, "Why did I break up with that girl? She was perfect for me."

The last major relationship I had, about a decade ago, was with Maria. I've had other girlfriends since then, but Maria was special because I was completely in love with her and she was in love with me, too. I had an episode between the time I asked her to be my girlfriend and the time I became full-blown manic. I got lucky with the timing because she accepted being my girlfriend before I got sick.

So, like a good girlfriend, she waited around for almost 20 days until I got better. We weren't allowed to see or speak to each other because my parents were making sure that I didn't mess things up. I couldn't understand this at the time. It was particularly strange because she lived in front of my parents' house, where I was being held against my will. I could literally see her from the backyard of my parent's house while going through all the stages of mania. First, comes the euphoria, which I had so much fun with because Maria and I actually spent that time together. She was blown away by my charisma and the amount of fun we were having. We actually got together once, took out white canvases, and started to paint. We did things like we were two little kids. Maria was compact and easy to carry, so I'd carry her on my back piggyback-style and run as fast as I could.

It was so much fun, but like all my episodes, I lost control of my sleep and started sleeping less and less until I devolved into the usual wreck. My parents took over and abducted me, holding me hostage in their house for a full dose of medicine and close observation. Maria meant a lot to me. We got over the episode together (but apart).

She showed me that I could love again, which was the most important thing I gained from being with her. Our relationship started going downhill when Maria started becoming overly obsessive and domineering. She became controlling to the point that our love started to wither away. She wasn't jealous—that was more me than her. However, she was super controlling and it started to cause me a lot of resentment. I mean, I thought of Maria and could hear church bells ringing. I loved her and wanted to marry her, but I couldn't spend my life with a woman who was so controlling. I realized that staying with her would mean that I would lose a lot of my own agency, and I wasn't willing to do that.

Maria was everything to me. I spent every waking hour, when I wasn't working, with her and her family. Her family also knew about Maria's demeanor and would say she had a Napoleon complex because she was short and bossy. One time, while kidding around, her father told me, "Hey if you get married to her, we don't accept returns." We would half-joke about the way she was.

Ending the relationship became a mission. On my first try at ending things, she simply said that she wouldn't accept it. I'd never been put in this type of situation. A normal girl just gets upset or cries and life goes on, but that wasn't Maria's style. She was deeply in love with me and I with her. It was her controlling attitude that I couldn't deal with.

Breaking up when you love someone is so much harder to do than with someone you care about but don't love. However, I had already made up my mind that staying with her was not going to be healthy. Someone who covets freedom to its maximum expression couldn't stay with someone like her. We talked about therapy, and my only thought was, *Therapy as boyfriend and girlfriend? We're not even married yet and we already need therapy? No way! That makes no sense to me, I'm sorry.*

One time, we were in my car and I abruptly stopped on the side of the road to talk to Maria. I told her that I was in love with her but that I was disillusioned with her controlling demeanor. I told her I couldn't see a marriage in our future, that I was really sorry, and had no intention of wasting her time. By this point in my life, I knew very well that people seldom change. Maybe evolve somewhat, but I knew that Maria wasn't going to change and that it would only get worse if we tied the knot.

I wondered to myself why I was wasting my time—or hers—and that I needed to cut my losses already. But, as I said, she wouldn't accept us breaking up. I then tried to take her home and she grabbed hold of the steering wheel. *Okay,* I thought to myself, *this is getting out of control.* I finally pleaded with her for us to take a timeout, she finally conceded, and I took her home.

By that time, I was living in my own apartment, so at least my parents didn't witness everything that went down. Maria came back the next day, pounding on my door to the point that she got a bruise on the side of her hand. The pounding was so strong that I decided I wasn't going to open the door. If she'd decided to come at me with that type of aggression, I wasn't having it. I quickly locked the door to my room and got back into bed, where I'd been peacefully watching Netflix.

To my surprise, Maria jumped the gate and snuck in through one of my windows. I could hear her footsteps as she came up the stairs, directly to my room. Again, a banging on the door. At this point, I wasn't sure if she was coming with a knife in her hand or what was going on. I decided to confront my fears, not knowing what was going to happen.

I opened up and Maria was sweeter than ever, but the first thing she did was grab my car keys. For some reason or another, this really set me off. I wrestled her for the keys, which is something I regret to this day because it was quite a scuffle. She didn't get hurt—and neither did I—but I got my keys back, only to open the door and see that she had parked her car perpendicular to mine, making it impossible for me to leave. *What was going on? What was I supposed to do?* This had never happened to me in my whole life.

I know she came into that room to seduce me. She crawled into my bed, and I knew I had to restrain myself from getting physical with her. This is hard for any man to do. I mean, a woman who wants you is next to you on your bed; it's a tough spot to be in. I figured out a way to get myself out of trouble by reaching over to my computer and asking Maria, "Hey, what would you like to watch?"

Bear in mind, I'm a Taurus, and even though I don't believe in astrology, I do agree that Taurus is a sign that is hard-headed and has a personality that once he makes up his mind, he doesn't change it. This strong-willed stubbornness has gotten me in trouble a thousand times over, but it's who I am. Bipolar disorder aside, I'm a guy set in his ways, and moving me from one opinion to try and convince me of another is almost impossible. I was ready to stay in bed watching Netflix for days, if necessary—that's how determined I was not to go back with her.

So, I stood strong. She understood that nothing physical was going to happen and then she showed me her hand. It was all bruised up, and I freaked out because I believed it to be something that was caused by the 10-second scuffle we'd had over the car keys. *I'm screwed*, I thought to myself. *This girl is going to go to her family and show them how I physically abused her.* This would be very bad for me, as I had a reputation for being soft and not rough with any girl I'd ever dated. I was freaking out until I pointed out the bruise and Maria explained that it was from banging so hard on the door. *Oh, man, what a relief.* Getting arrested for abusing a woman did not appeal to me.

After about two hours, Maria finally clued into the fact that I wasn't going to make a move to have makeup sex—or any sex—with her. I stood my ground like a stubborn bull and didn't allow for anything to take place between us.

It took me years to get over Maria. Other girls who came after her could tell I wasn't fully over her because I wasn't. I truly loved her, but I had to protect myself from a bad combination. As a person with bipolar disorder, I can tell you that freedom is something super-important to us. If you've ever been tied to a bed, you would understand why being with someone who is obsessively controlling would be a non-starter.

I've spent quality time tied to beds during at least half of my manic episodes and can confirm how awful it is. So, being free while we're not sick, which is 99% of the time, is more than paramount. It is non-negotiable. It makes me sad to reminisce about how much I loved this girl. Hugging her was like being in heaven; it always felt so right. In hindsight, maybe I made too much of a big deal about the control issue. But, hey, I was just trusting my gut, which is what I always do. Maybe I need to trust my gut a little less. Who knows?

# Chapter 25:

# Understanding Myself

With time, I've grown to understand myself and my bipolar condition. I have a lot of triggers that can provoke manic episodes. Overstimulation is a big-time trigger. For example, until I was about 40, I loved commemorating my birthday, which is in May. I would usually put on a grand production and invite loads of friends to celebrate with me. This was clearly a trigger, and today I'm well aware that throwing parties where there are 100+ people present is not a good idea.

Another trigger is drinking alcohol in heavy doses. If I drink three or four drinks a night, that's probably okay, but when I go out and drink to get plastered, I'm playing with fire. Alcohol can not only trigger mania, but it can also cause severe hangovers that make me feel utterly depressed and almost suicidal. It's hard to believe, but smoking cigarettes in large quantities can also contribute to a manic episode.

Sometimes, I'm a bit confused on this topic. It's a chicken-and-egg quagmire. I don't know if smoking causes me to get manic or if once I feel a little manic, I start to chain-smoke, which only further exacerbates the episode. It's not uncommon for me to smoke two packs of cigarettes per day when I'm fully manic. I don't know what it is, but smoking is incredibly delicious when I'm on a euphoric high. I became a cigarette junky.

But the truth is, I don't look for alcohol when I'm manic. The worst trigger of all is one that I have no control over: girls. When I become infatuated with a girl and I can't get her out of my mind, I kick off an obsessive cycle that will run out of control if not put in check. This is maddening because, when I really like a girl, I usually end up tied to a bed—and not by her, mind you, but by the psychiatric ward at a hospital. I'm 46 years old as I write this, and if it weren't for my obstructive manic episodes when I fall head over heels for a woman, I probably would've gotten married a long time ago. My condition is a tough pill to swallow for the better half I have yet to find.

I live in a small community where everyone knows one another. I've always been an open book about my condition. I don't know if that's been the smartest way to go about it. If I could do it again, I would probably be a little more careful with this information, because, on top of being a small community, it's plagued with prejudice and taboo. For example, being gay is still a huge deal in Nicaragua. My older brother William, who is openly gay, suffered a tremendous amount of prejudice. He ultimately settled in Brazil, where being gay is almost as remarkable as being left-handed.

There's another trigger, and this one is a no-brainer: Stress and not sleeping well for long periods of time will always hasten the emergence of a manic episode. This has become a major challenge for me. I can't sleep today without taking large quantities of meds. At bedtime, I take 600 mg of Seroquel and down it with 4 mgs of Clonazepam. Sometimes, if that doesn't knock me out, I'll round out the snooze cocktail with 50 mgs of Clozapine.

Over my lifespan (I was diagnosed at 17) as someone who lives with bipolar disorder, I've had many more euphoric (manic) episodes than depressive episodes. This is pretty easy to explain. As I mentioned before, when I see the tail of the dragon, I immediately look for help. The type of help I usually get is in the form of antidepressants. One that has worked especially well for me is Lexapro, otherwise known as Escitalopram or Cipralex.

I know when I'm starting to get symptoms of depression, so I always act fast and let my doctor know how I'm feeling. If you feel symptoms of depression coming on, don't wait to see your doctor; instead, call them and let them know you're going to start taking antidepressants. In my case, I already know my go-to antidepressant is Lexapro, but drugs affect everyone differently. Also, some people might have a load of side effects from certain types of antidepressants. If you have to see your doctor, make sure to say that it's an emergency and you must meet within a week. There's no reason for anyone to suffer any type of depression because they couldn't get to the doctor on time. As a person with bipolar disorder, you must always be vigilant of "the tail of the dragon." You must never allow depression to get the best of you.

Now, when it comes to treating my manic episodes, that is far trickier. The problem lies in the fact that, when I'm manic, I am therefore feeling great. No one looks for help when they're on top of the world. It's silly to even expect someone in a manic state to look for help. You probably won't. You'll probably want to ride that wave for as long as it lasts. This will eventually become a disruptive nuisance for those around you, at which point you are most likely going to have to be committed by force.

The most descriptive example of me being forced to capitulate was a manic episode I had in Austin during my Master's program. I had a euphoric episode out of sheer joy about the program I was studying, but it ended up being too stressful and started affecting my sleep. I had the episode during my first semester, so my sister had to come down from Washington, DC, where she had settled after graduation, to take care of me. She did everything she could, which included calling the paramedics to come to her aide.

When they saw me, they didn't spot any reason why I should be committed, so I got away with that one. However, that night, at 4:00 a.m., my sister called my parents in Managua. I was wide awake and blasting music, as I tend to do when I'm on a high. My family was running out of ideas about what to do, so they ended up telling Catalina to call the police and tell them I had threatened her life. Of course, this was untrue, but it was the best she could do.

I'll never forget hanging out by the pool of my apartment complex when two policemen showed up in a cop car. The first cop was super antagonistic and screamed at me to get out of the pool. I yelled back, not understanding what was going on. After all, I'm not super-aggressive when I'm manic—or, at least, I don't think I am. The second police guy, who towered over me and was much older than the first cop, came onto the pool deck. He sat me down and made me feel safe. He said that I was going to be taken away in handcuffs but that everything was going to be alright. I deposited a great deal of trust in this man as he put the cuffs on my wrists. He felt like a father figure I could trust with my life.

I had never worn handcuffs in my life, and I can now tell you that it hurts like hell. What you have to do is try and clasp your hands together as much as possible to minimize the pain. You figure this out pretty quickly when you're put in this position. I was escorted to the back of the car very gently; it wasn't aggressive or brutish. It was more like I was walking slowly to the patrol car and put it in the back very gently. There was certainly no feeling of police brutality, mostly because I didn't fight back. However, I did open the plastic window that communicated with the front of the patrol car with my nose because I felt like I couldn't breathe.

It was such a horrible feeling. I was being treated like a criminal when all I was doing was having a good time in the pool—a really good time. That was the problem. Catalina was in tears as she watched the police haul me away—after all, she had no idea what they were going to do to me.

# Chapter 26:

# Dating and Noncompliance

There's definitely something confusing about being bipolar and trying to create lasting relationships with girlfriends. This is a fiendishly difficult arena to navigate, so I'll try to express my difficulty with this subject as best I can.

For all who suffer from mental illness, it's a tough thing to bring up when you're in the process of courting a significant other. It's not exactly first-date material. But, seriously, when's the appropriate time to tell a person that you sometimes feel like Jesus' brother, or Jesus himself? Or, that sometimes you can't sleep for a week and you go past a euphoric episode into one of chaotic psychosis? After all, anyone with bipolar disorder is going to have manic states that can be difficult to navigate with your life partner. If the relationship doesn't have a strong foundation, many women will simply run for the hills.

See, I think bipolar disorder is more of a sleep disorder than a mental one. Any human being deprived of sleep for four or five days will most likely suffer some form of psychosis that will end up transforming reality and become a scary scenario for a partner who is experiencing what it's like to be with someone who is fully manic. On top of all those things, many people with bipolar disorder suffer from some sort of issue with their thyroid gland, which somehow manages to add greater complexity to the whole situation.

All of this is hard to take in for someone you're potentially dating or want to date. So, when's the right time to tell your loved one that you suffer from crippling depression, soaring heights of euphoria, and potentially psychotic states? Not exactly the easiest bomb to drop on a person. I don't think there's a clear answer to this question. In my case, I've tried to wait until we've been dating for at least three months before I begin to tell my significant other about my dark secret.

Mental health should not be a taboo subject these days, but I believe it still is, especially in backward traditional societies such as Nicaragua's, and coming out of that closet remains a huge challenge for those who are either unipolar, suffering only from the downs, or Bipolar I or II. People with Bipolar I suffer from more ups than downs; whereas, those with Bipolar II suffer more downs than ups. Both manic and depressive states will have potentially devastating effects on your relationships with your loved ones.

Depression, for example, is something that I've experienced to its darkest expression. Since the first manifestation of my bipolar condition came with a paralyzing and grim depression that lasted more than three months, I'm intimately aware of what depression is and what it feels like. A person in this state can make very unwise decisions and fall into a state of despair, which can lead to suicide.

In my opinion, not enough credence is given to depression and/or mental disorders in general. In my mind, depression is as dangerous as cancer because both can kill when left untreated. According to the World Health Organization (2023), one in every eight people in the world live with a mental disorder. They consider a mental disorder something that involves significant disturbances in thinking, emotional regulation, or behavior. That's 12.5% of the world's population. It should be taken much more seriously than it is. The WHO also says that more than 700,000 people commit suicide every year. For every suicide, many more people attempt it. It is the fourth-leading cause of death among 15 to 29-year-olds.

The first depression is the most dangerous. The red dragon turns into a python that overpowers and suffocates you until you finally capitulate and fall into a deep chasm with no way out. It's like a parasite that takes over both your mind and your body. It's there to take away all hope and make you feel, instead, like a burden to those around you. Logical thinking along the lines of "This is just a stage; it will go away" does not happen.

You see no light at the end of the tunnel, and life begins taking on less and less meaning as the python pulls you slowly underwater, where there are no bubbles of hope. You lose all sense of well-being, and your self-esteem is squandered and replaced with only doubts and slow, paralyzing agony. Your sexual urges disappear. In my case, I stopped eating and showering for weeks at a time. I missed a lot of school, and when I did go to school, it felt like a punishment. I wouldn't wish this state on anyone.

Today, it's truly one of the reasons that I ask myself whether I want to bring a child into this world, knowing that I might pass this condition on to them. According to the Depression and Bipolar Support Alliance, a huge foundation with their main headquarters in Chicago, "For mood disorders like depression and bipolar disorder, genes are an important risk factor." However, your genes are certainly not your destiny. "On average, the risk of developing bipolar disorder is less than 1% (or about one person out of 120). For people who have a parent with bipolar disorder, the risk is 8% (or about one person out of 12)…" Even if your child would be 10 times as likely to develop bipolar disorder as the average person, there is still a greater than 90% chance that she or he would not develop bipolar disorder (DBSA, n.d.).

I'm not sure I want to play those odds. Though there are times when I thank God he made me the way I am, there are also an equal amount of times when I can't stand living with this dark passenger. The condition is something you can't escape. Even if you're following all the instructions and taking your meds exactly as prescribed, you will still have ups and downs. And, that doesn't even account for the scars you invariably inflict in your personal relationships and professional career, whose lingering effects may not heal so easily, even if you spend the rest of your life under control.

At least, in my case, counting from my first manic episode, in 1997, I've had at least 9 or more manic episodes over the last 29 years, putting me at around an episode every 3 years. I hardly count the depressions because, as I mentioned before, I'm quick to recognize the tail of the dragon or the early onset of a major depression. I am always looking for help right away and usually start a regimen of antidepressants before even consulting my doctor. It's not something I completely recommend, but sometimes desperate times call for desperate measures—and there is no reason on earth why you should suffer one more day of an unnecessary depressive state when there is so much technology out there that can help you slay your dark passenger, your red-tailed dragon.

There's one thing that I do have to admit to myself. I've had continuous problems throughout my life with noncompliance, which is basically a disregard for taking the medicine you are prescribed. This phenomenon is quite common when it comes to people with mental health issues. We just don't want to take our meds. They make us feel strange and cause us to feel the stigma of not being normal like everyone else. For me, I've felt fine at several points in my life, which led me to wean off of Lithium several times.

Noncompliance is one of the biggest challenges to helping people find mental balance and a stable lifestyle. "In 35 studies conducted (schizophrenia = 9 studies), (depressive = 16 studies), and (bipolar = 10 studies), the meta-analysis concluded that overall, 49% of major psychiatric disorder patients were non-adherent to their psychotropic medication... Individual patients' behaviors, lack of social support, clinical or treatment, and illness-related and health system factors influenced psychotropic medication nonadherence" (Semahegn et al., 2020).

Alcohol abuse was also a common thing for me. I lived most of my adolescent years in Nicaragua, where I started drinking as early as ninth grade, at the tender age of 14. I clearly remember my first time getting drunk. My parents were out of town, and I threw a house party with all my closest guy friends. We didn't know what we were doing. None of us really had a lot of experience with alcohol.

I think for most of us that night was the first time we had white rum, and we drank it straight. We all got obliterated and had a blast. A lot of the fun centered on the fact we were in a safe place and doing something our parents would never have allowed us to do. In 1993, when this all happened, there really was nothing for us, as teenagers, to do in Nicaragua. There were probably three or four restaurants in Managua at the time, but there were no movie theaters or malls. There wasn't even one fast-food franchise in the whole country.

After all, Nicaragua was just waking up from a 10-year hiatus from normal economic activity. The roads were peppered with potholes, and the country was handed over pretty much in a state of abject bankruptcy. It was so bad, in fact, that the government at that time decided to take apart the railroad system and sell off the steel and girders from the tracks so they could source more operating capital. I still believe this was a huge setback for a country that had a railroad system that connected all its major cities where over 70% of the population lived.

I understand that we had fallen on tough times, but I believe that dismantling the railroad was a ham-fisted, shortsighted thing to do. But who knows the difficulty that the government was facing? Having said all that, I guess I really can't give a fair assessment of what happened with the railroad since I was hardly 12 when this took place.

As a result of a country trying to move forward as a newly democratic republic, there weren't many things for teenagers to do. I started going out to bars when I was only in 10th grade. No IDs were required at the front of the line. The '80s was considered "the lost decade." It was a time when the United States covertly waged war on Nicaragua as Nicaragua sought out support from countries like Cuba and the USSR. From what I've read and studied, the revolution to overthrow the Somoza dynasty (a violent dictatorship that lasted three generations) was an interesting time. I don't want to get political, so I will stick to the facts.

In the '80s, the US withdrew support for the post-dictatorship Nicaraguan government, mostly because of its relationship with the Soviet Union and the fact that the revolutionary Sandinista government was actively spreading revolution over to El Salvador—something that the Americans had warned them against. Whether you were pro or anti-government didn't matter. The fact was that the United States was funding a counter-revolution without the consent of the U.S. Congress. These counterinsurgents were called the Contras and were based mainly in neighboring Honduras. That, coupled with a trade embargo and, perhaps, some government mismanagement of funds due to corruption and inexperience, obliterated the economy of Nicaragua— hence, the lost decade.

According to Photius Coutsoukis (2005), the GDP in Nicaragua between 1984 and 1990 dropped substantially. "Between decreasing revenues, mushrooming military expenditures, and printing large amounts of paper money, inflation peaked at 14,000% annually in 1987." The country was a basket case in 1990, when it was turned over to the conservative government led by Violeta Chamorro, the first female elected president in all of Latin America. She was also the widow of the famous Nicaraguan martyr I mentioned earlier in this book, Pedro Joaquin Chamorro.

Chamorro's administration was able to broker peace and stability among the country's different political factions, a difficult task that she took on as the war came to a close in the early '90s. Peace efforts were primarily brokered by Costa Rican president Oscar Arias, for which he was awarded the Nobel Peace Prize in 1987.

# Chapter 27:

# Family and Peer Support

I don't know where I would be if I hadn't had all the support from family and friends—specifically, family because they were the ones who had to deal with a manic Joshua, something that requires oodles of patience. When I'm manic, I become like a child who just wants to play or, on the opposite end of the spectrum, an elder with deep prophetic knowledge of the universe.

I consider myself a nonviolent manic, but I'm not sure that is the norm. Being manic gives you superhuman strength. That's part of the reason it usually takes about three big, injection-wielding orderlies to get me committed. It's happened so many times that now my thought process is, "Okay, you got me. I give up." Once I get a glimpse of the orderlies approaching, I don't even try to run away. I just allow them to grab me and anxiously await the sting of the injection.

I have to mention, one by one, all the love and support that I've had from my family as a deep thank you for not allowing my illness to take over my life. My mother is first. She is a very special woman. She's always the first one to notice when I'm acting a little off, and she's always asking me not to drink alcohol, or if I do, to do it in moderation. My mother has spent time with me during so many episodes, and I'm sure it breaks her heart to a million pieces to see me forcibly tied to a bed. Since my mother is the one who knows the most about me, she actually becomes enemy number one, because I know she's on to me and that means the party's over. She's suffered the most because of my condition and I love her so much, to the moon and back, for all she's done for me.

Another special mention is to my brother, William, who, as it turns out, is also bipolar. His experience with me in Japan was enough to drive anyone mad. I can't imagine the stress he went through. He's my hero in so many ways. When I was down in my first and only suicidal depression, he was the one who kept me going and kept believing in me. Without him, I never would have attended the University of Michigan, where he had studied a year before I attended.

William suffered greatly when they put me in the public psychiatric facility in Costa Rica, the first time I was committed. William, you are my bipolar twin and I know that together we have been defeating our dark passenger. It's actually kind of crazy because I once had to call on two military attachés to take William violently out of his house and to a hospital. I was the one who had them in the car and I was the one who decided to call the code red. ("Code red" comes from *A Few Good Men*, one of our favorite movies. "Did you order a code red?"…"You're goddamn right I did!") To this day, we let each other know when we're starting to get noticed by the Queen Bee, my mother.

"William, chill the fuck out, you don't want my mom to call a code red." "You need to stop partying and take a two-day nap." We always joke about the code red; it's something that binds us—something we share only with each other.

A special mention goes to my younger sister, Catalina, who had to babysit me in Austin, Texas, of all places. She had to take a week or more off work and fly down from DC to find a manic brother, who was already in the throes of full-blown psychosis. I will never forget all that you did for me, little sis. You saved my life. I also want to mention my brother, Francisco, and his wife, Jessica. They live up the street in Managua, so they are kind of on-call with me in regard to my mental health. You guys have been very supportive, and I appreciate every second you have taken to protect me and take care of me.

Last, but not least, is my father. He's my greatest ally when I'm sick. Our relationship deepens as my relationship with the motherload decreases substantially. My family already knows that it's my father who needs to take care of me the most when I'm sick. His gentle words and non-confrontational demeanor are what set him apart from the rest of my family. I'll never forget how you froze your ass off in the middle of -40°F weather to take care of your little boy, your lithium kid.

In the end, being bipolar is a gift, but it comes with a lot of challenges. Looking for support from family and friends is key. All my friends know of my condition and none of them judge me for it. They're always looking out for me, making sure I am not like Icarus, who fell from the sky because he flew too close to the sun.

It is my wish to share this book with all who suffer from mental illness. It's an invisible disease that is severely misunderstood. Never give up hope for a better and more stable day. Just when you think your red-tailed dragon can't get any worse, he too will be vanquished. Use the technology and use the medicine. It's there to help you, not harm you—and yes, it's not 100% bulletproof, but wouldn't you rather fight a war with a hard hat and a vest? I know I would. Oh, about the mole on my butt—there's no story about it. I just said it to keep you in suspense! Hahaha.

# Afterword

Today, I'm alone and it's not a great place to be when living in contemporary Nicaragua. The country is endowed with beautiful colonial cities, volcanoes, lagoons, and beaches that are all way better when you have someone to share them with.

Finding a mate has been difficult for me as I've had a hell of a time staying stable. Just as an example: During the writing of this book, I suffered through a mild depression, a hypomanic episode, and a full-blown manic episode. I just haven't been able to find the balance I need.

Since the last manic episode, I've decided no more drinking and no more smoking cigarettes. Both clearly set me off. I've realized that I don't need either of those bad habits in my life. The fewer chemicals I put in my body, the better. Not being able to drink is going to be tough because, in my country, most social events revolve around imbibing. But, I will borrow the creed that is put forth at AA: "One day at a time."

The right girl will eventually come at some point, but for now, I think I need to take care of myself. Exercise regularly, focus on work, try to wake up early and at the same time every day, and set some goals to accomplish and make them happen.

Overall, I would like for everyone who reads this book, whether you're someone suffering from a mental disorder or have a loved one who might be suffering, to take mental illness as something that is real. Even though it's virtually an invisible disease for those who don't have it, those who are healthy mentally must try and be as empathetic and positive as possible, there is real suffering taking place, especially when it comes to depression.

For those who suffer from bipolar disorder, try to be aware of how difficult things are for those who are on the other side of your manic episodes. It is emotionally draining to have to take care of a child or adult in a full-blown manic state. I also recognize how difficult it is to have your loved one committed, but most of the time, depending on the level of psychosis (which usually comes after the euphoria), getting them into the hospital is usually the best choice. You don't want your manic loved one to make bad financial decisions or allow them to become violent or confrontational—or just make poor decisions, in general.

I am a big proponent of going to the psych ward, which is hard to believe coming from a guy who deals with manic depression all of the time and enjoys euphoria like everyone else who has lived through this type of mental state. I urge everyone who has a mental illness, especially those who suffer from depression, to seek help quickly.

The more experience you have with depression will help you recognize when a depressive state is starting to happen. Be swift and make decisions quickly; go to your doctor and have them prescribe the right antidepressant for you. As I said before, it will be different for different people. I want to hammer this home for everyone who deals with depression: There is no reason you should suffer in silence; always look for help. The meds are there for you to make use of them, when necessary. They can help you.

As for those who live with someone who has whatever type of mental illness they might have, try as much as you can to be as supportive as possible. Those with loved ones affected by mental health should also know that nothing is permanent and, sometimes, you will have to make appointments with the doctor when the mental illness is too strong.

In the end, I wrote this book as a testament to mental illness survival. I hope it is a legacy piece that will help those in need of it, whether you have a mental illness or live with someone who does. Be kind and understanding to those who suffer from this. It is not their fault that they have a mental illness.

Since my older brother is also bipolar, I have had the unique opportunity to be on the other side, which has taught me so much about how much I appreciate all my loved ones who have been there for me through the toughest times. I leave you with these famous words from my mother: "Everything has a solution but death."

Ultimately, I would like to thank God for putting all the guardian angels in my way through the adventurous path that led me to mental health enlightenment. I also give thanks to God for giving me the maturity to not only accept my illness but embrace it and share my knowledge of it with others.

Overall, I urge people to get involved and to offer support when someone they know is affected by whatever mental disorder comes their way. This goes for both those with mental illness, as well as those who live with someone who does. Always remember: No matter how dark it feels, there is a light at the end of the tunnel.

***For ways to get in touch with a large organization that offers great support to those suffering from mental illness, I suggest checking out www.dbsalliance.org***

# About the Author



Joshua C. Campo is a philanthropist and an avid advocate of mental health awareness. He graduated from the University of Michigan with degrees in both Political Science and History. In his spare time, he enjoys reading fictional historical novels, swimming, and playing chess. Joshua currently lives in Managua, Nicaragua.

jcldigibook@gmail.com

# Resources

Boyle, K. (2001, April 30). *Arc of justice: A saga of race, civil rights, and murder in the Jazz Age*. Holt Paperbacks.

Coutsoukis, P. (2005, March 5). *Nicaragua inflation*. Photius. https://photius.com/countries/nicaragua/economy/nicaragua _economy_inflation.html

Depression and Bipolar Support Alliance. (n.d.). *Bipolar disorder statistics*. https://www.dbsalliance.org/education/bipolar-disorder/bipolar-disorder-statistics/

*Hope is the last to die*. (n.d.). Detroit's Great Rebellion. http://www.detroits-great-rebellion.com/Post-Riot-Detroit.html

Semahegn, A., Torpey, K., Manu, A., Assefa, N., Tesfaye, G., & Ankomah, A. (2020, January 16). Psychotropic medication non-adherence and its associated factors among patients with major psychiatric disorders: A systematic review and meta-analysis. *Systematic Reviews, 9*(1). https://doi.org/10.1186/s13643-020-1274-3

Sugrue, T. J. (2005). *The origins of the urban crisis: Race and inequality in postwar Detroit*. Princeton University Press.

Sugrue, T. J. (2014, September 16). *Motor City: The story of Detroit*. The Gilder Lehrman Institute of American History. http://gdelaurier.pbworks.com/w/file/fetch/85732135/Motor%20City_%20The%20Story%20of.pdf

World Health Organization. (2023, August 28). *Suicide*. https://www.who.int/news-room/fact-sheets/detail/suicide

Williamson, M. (2014, December 15). *Detroit: Decline and fall of the Motor City*. Engineering and Technology Magazine. https://eandt.theiet.org/2014/12/15/detriot-decline-and-fall-motor-city